Worship, What Have We Been Missing?

James F. Wingerter

Published by Tzemach Institute for Biblical Studies, P.O. Box 181191, Casselberry, Florida 32718.   Website: http://www.BuildUpZion.org Questions to the author may be sent to the mailing address above or via email at: jim@FaceOfGodmusic.com

ISBN 978-0-9669174-1-3
Library of Congress Control Number: 2010921756

Unless otherwise stated, all Scripture quotations are taken from the *New American Standard Bible* Copyright © 1960, 1962, 1963, 1968, 1971, 1972, 1973, 1975, 1977 by The Lockman Foundation. Used by permission.

Table of Contents

ACKNOWLEDGMENTS

Beginning decades ago with commonly-known foundational concepts of worship, I believe the Lord has procured in us a more developed understanding, which has been discovered and realized in the experience of the congregation of Fellowship Church, where I have served as Minister of Music for the past sixteen years. I would like to thank the congregation who has been bold in spirit and strong in faith to venture forth in this discovery process. The early work was established before I came on board, and was a direct result of the efforts and direction given by Pastor Ken Garrison, his wife, pianist and song writer, Jorene Garrison, and song leader Larry Dorcik. In addition, I would like to express thanks to the many individuals who contributed directly to the preparation of this work: Pastor Ken Garrison, Pastor Roger Diaz, Associate Pastor Jon Klein, Mary Benedick and Jim Dibbley for their work in reviewing and proofreading the text. A special thank you to John Hellein for direction in layout and assistance in the clarity of the presentation. Finally, I would like to thank my wife, Linda, for her perseverance while experiencing much of the basis for this work alongside myself and for her encouragement in the long process of compiling and writing this text.

James F. Wingerter

INTRODUCTION

There are some good things happening in the world of Christian music today, but there are also a fair number of things that are frankly strange. As *pastors* build *mega-churches* (a worldly measure of success) we are led to believe that bigger is better. In many cases what is called "worship" is really just an entertaining show. I believe there are no spectators in God's kingdom. It is, therefore, the intent of this book to provide worship leaders and individual members of congregations tools that will assist and encourage a fuller participation in the Kingdom of God.

There are a number of very good books that deal analytically with biblical praise and worship, but for musicians (and non-musicians) they are equivalent to sleeping pills. It may be better to just read the scriptures, but that requires word studies they have done for you in those books. The best I have found, and would therefore recommend, is called the Divine Habitation Trilogy by Kevin J. Conner.

My further intent in this book is to take up where the scholars have left off by rolling up our sleeves, combining their scholarly concepts with the guidance of the Lord and plowing ahead into what, in this age, appears to be uncharted territory.

It is my hope that you will prayerfully read and implement the steps outlined in this book and that the Lord will bring a fresh and bold anointing in His Church through you while we remain in this present age.

James F. Wingerter
Minister of Music
Fellowship Church
Casselberry, Florida

1. What Have We Been Missing?

"James!" My mother's voice startled me out of yet another daydream I had fallen into in the middle of putting on my black dress shoes (worn only on Sunday mornings and for special occasions). "I don't want to be late for worship. Your father insists we set an example for the congregation, so we have to be early." I tied my shoes and slid down the back steps, followed by Mom. As we quickly traverse down the sidewalk along Analomink Street in East Stroudsburg, Pennsylvania en route to the Presbyterian Church where my Dad was Pastor, images from a murder mystery depicting occult worship I had recently seen on television came to mind. Worship... what was the connection between the few songs we were about to sing and these images of the dark side I now held in my mind? If there was no connection, why were they both called worship?

To be sure, I was proud of most everything we did from week-to-week and the structure of our worship services was a source of comfort. But as a young boy I began to question my experience. As elementary and unformulated as my thinking was at that time, I wondered how the worship services I grew up knowing had evolved from the worship I saw in the Scriptures: Israel at Mount Sinai; Saul prophesying; David bringing the Ark of the Covenant to Jerusalem.

Years later (as a college student) I was sitting in the middle of another "worship" service in a Baptist Church north of Tallahassee, Florida. We had just finished an altar call, singing the famous hymn "Just as I Am," which (after a few weeks I had realized) was a weekly ritual. Light filtered through stained and clear glass above to my left and right. Ushers moved to their positions with offering plates in hand. Inside my head, a song started:

"Is that all there is?"

Someone up front was making an announcement but Peggy Lee would not be interrupted.

"Is that all there is? If that's all there is my friends, then let's keep dancing. Let's break out the booze and have a ball, if that's all there is."

My Christian experience - and the experience of every Christian I knew - had boiled down to this: a few songs, an offering, a morning prayer and a sermon. Looking back, I have a better perspective on just how processed, preserved and boiled my Christian experience had become. At the time, of course, I was still in the pot, boiling.

Peggy Lee's song became a cry in my heart: "Is that all there is?" I began to read the Bible and found my perception of the gap between those accounts and my experience ever widening. Some years later I took my family to visit a "Shabbat" service held by a "Messianic" congregation in Fort Lauderdale, Florida. At that time their entire service appeared to me to be remarkably different from what I considered to be normal worship. My first response was that they were doing it all wrong, but after considering the origins of the world religion of Christianity against the much earlier origins of Judaism, I concluded that it was conceivable that these "Jewish believers in Jesus (Yeshua)" may well be worshiping as their father Abraham had worshiped. I was intrigued.

Merely months later, following a genuine revelation experience in Jesus I visited a worship service at a church where the enthusiasm for a corporate, full-congregation encounter with God was evident. As with other congregations I had visited, everything was different from what I had known while growing up, but I liked what I saw, that is, the worship this group experienced struck a note within me. I wanted it to be right even if I thought it was probably just another worship service like all of those I had experienced before.

Needless to say, that first visit was not the last. In fact, I have kept coming back for nearly twenty years now. The Lord heard my cry and, even though I did not realize it, He was orchestrating my life to provide the answer. He brought me to a congregation where every worship service is a challenge to every participant to interact, as a body, with the Living God. Along the way, thanks to a solid emphasis on Bible teaching in the congregation, we have come to embrace a wonderful vision or map of Biblical praise and worship that is no longer boiled down; instead, it is rooted in the Scriptures, bearing fruit as a vine in His vineyard. We have not arrived, but look forward each service to growing and to knowing more about Him and to participating in His awesome process of Redemption during these exciting days.

If you find yourself asking the question, "Is this all there is?" then let me say that this book is for you. It is not a coincidence - any more than it was a coincidence that I walked into Fellowship Church in Central Florida in 1991 - that you are reading these words. If you have been asking that question, then I pray that this book is part of His answer to you. Certainly, there will be challenges ahead and the book itself will likely challenge your perspective just as I found myself challenged; but equipped with a Biblical perspective on who you are and what you were called to do as a part of the body of Messiah, you will face those challenges without Peggy Lee nagging you in the middle of "worship."

The Pattern Before

Looking more closely at the "garden" experience we can see that Adam and Eve met God *"in the cool of the day,"*[1] clearly implying open communication with God occurred every day. It also seems apparent that they enjoyed unending life as they ate from the tree of life. God blessed all of nature through man.[2] We can also see that when they sinned they experienced emotions they had never before had any reason to know. They immediately recognized their state of nakedness (implying *inadequacy*) and they were ashamed. Although they may have been covered with the "glory of God," [3] they had always been physically naked [4] but had never before felt inadequate.

---

[1] Genesis 3:8
[2] Genesis 1:28: 2:19-20a
[3] Exodus 34:35; Revelation 19:8
[4] Genesis 2:25

With the question being raised *"Who told you that you were naked?"* it is apparent that there has been established a newly opened line of communication with the accuser.[5] They also hid themselves, and Adam for the first time in his life expressed *fear*, the fear of God's response to their *rebellion*.[6]

Beyond what we are given in the scripture, we can only speculate what life may have been like before the fall. God provided everything and they communed with Him daily. There was no sickness, disease or death. They had no reason to ever experience any of the multitudes of negative emotions we now deal with regularly. There had never been any strife between them and no one had ever done anything to hurt, insult or offend them in any way. The first time one offended another it must have been like small children playing and one takes something away from another, usually wanting the toy only because the other child has it. If it was the first time that happened to a child they don't fight back, they just stand there and cry hoping some adult will intervene and make justice.

It also seems likely that the struggle many people have today with addiction to euphoria-producing drugs may stem from a deeply rooted soul remembrance of our life "in the loins of Adam"[7] prior to the fall, and that the enemy is able to devour many of these individuals (drug-abusers) with this counterfeit euphoria. If we worship Him in spirit and in

---

[5] Revelation 12:9-10
[6] Genesis 3:10
[7] Hebrews 7:5-10

truth,[8] surely we can experience at least a portion or earnest of the "euphoria" Adam and Eve knew, standing in the presence of God.

The Pattern After

What we then see in the book of Revelation is a much fuller picture of worship, now specifically before "the thrones." [9] A great deal of worship is presented in this book. Since the ultimate polarization is being brought to completion, worship of God, the beast, and the attempted worship of an angel are presented. Those who are identified as the worshipers are "living creatures," elders, multitudes of people, angels and, of course, the apostle John. It is safe to assume it is everyone who is there. In their presentation they cast their crowns before the throne,[10] speak words of praise and worship, clothed in white robes they hold palm branches in their hands and cry out with a loud voice,[11] and they fall on their faces before the throne.[12] When all are shouting collectively it resembles

> *"the voice of a great multitude and the sound of many waters and like the sound of mighty peals of thunder..."* [13]

---

[8] John 4:23-24
[9] Revelation 20:4
[10] Revelation 4:10
[11] Revelation 7:9-10: 11:15
[12] Revelation 7:11; 11:16
[13] Revelation 19:6

These individuals are not holding back for anything and clearly are not concerned about being reverent in church! Although we can worship God just because He is God, there are specific reasons for why they are worshiping as they are.

> *"Worthy are You, our Lord and our God, to receive glory and honor and power; for (**because**) You created all things, and because of Your will they existed, and were created."* [14]

> *Then one of the elders answered, saying to me, "These who are clothed in the white robes, who are they, and where have they come from?" I said to him, "My lord, you know." And he said to me, "These are the ones who come out of the great tribulation, and they have washed their robes and made them white in the blood of the Lamb. "**For this reason**, they are before the throne of God; and they serve Him day and night in His temple; and He who sits on the throne will spread His tabernacle over them."* [15]

> *And the twenty-four elders, who sit on their thrones before God, fell on their faces and worshiped God, saying, "We give You thanks, O Lord God, the Almighty, who is and who was, **because** You have taken Your great power and have begun to reign."* [16]

---

[14] Revelation 4:11
[15] Revelation 7:13-15
[16] Revelation 11:16-17

After these things I heard something like a loud voice of a great multitude in heaven, saying, "Hallelujah! Salvation and glory and power belong to our God; **BECAUSE** *HIS JUDGMENTS ARE TRUE AND RIGHTEOUS; for He has judged the great harlot who was corrupting the earth with her immorality, and HE HAS AVENGED THE BLOOD OF HIS BOND-SERVANTS ON HER."* [17]

*"Let us rejoice and be glad and give the glory to Him, for (**because**) the marriage of the Lamb has come and His bride has made herself ready." It was given to her to clothe herself in fine linen, bright and clean; for the fine linen is the righteous acts of the saints.* [18]

It is not surprising that there are many, many songs that have been written using quotes from these sections that identify worship before the throne. If you read through them in your bible, you will probably find yourself singing some of them in your head as you read through the texts. Notice that not just in these verses, but also throughout the bible, most often the term "worshiped God" is preceded by "fell down" or "prostrated." The whole picture is awesomely profound and vastly different from what most of us have experienced in "church."

The Pattern for Now

Awesome as both the garden experience and the completion of God's work of redemption are to consider, and although they represent our ultimate goal, they do not represent where we are now. Our challenge then is to

---

[17] Revelation 19:1-2
[18] Revelation 19:7-8

perceive our role as the body of the Messiah (Christ) in this time. Jesus told us:

> *"Truly, truly, I say to you, he who believes in Me, the works that I do, he will do also; and greater works than these he will do; because I go to the Father."* [19]

A development that occurred in the early church is the concept of functioning as Jesus' body on the earth. Jesus introduced the concept of His body being manifested through an assembled group of people,[20] but the apostle Paul defines it much further, since he was the chosen vessel of establishing a number of the first churches. One of those churches was in Corinth, which is in Greece, west of Athens. In writing a letter to that church he defines the "body" in great detail.[21] Is it possible that the fulfillment of what Jesus was talking about when He said *"the works that I do, he will do also; and greater works than these he will do; because I go to the Father"* was meant to be through assembled bodies, and not through stand-alone individuals who are (as with us all) easily promoted and idolized? We can surely see a great deal of this idolatry in the world of *televangelism* today. It is good that these televangelists believe God will use them and for many they are exercising faith for His manifestation through them, but the apostle Paul made it clear that we are the body of Jesus and therefore no part of that body can stand alone. Jesus being the "head" makes the decisions for how the body will function and what it (His body) will do. We are made to be dependent on one another in order that He might be manifested through us.

---

[19] John 14:12
[20] John 2:19-21; Matthew 18:20
[21] 1 Corinthians 12 & 14

Why did He go to be with the Father? Why would He not have been resurrected and continued to remain here on earth? We could easily consider that His goals would have been more effectively fulfilled if over the last two thousand years He had remained here continuing His ministry throughout all that time. How awesome it would be if we could arrange a special meeting with Jesus as our guest speaker! In the awesome wisdom of the Father, however, He determined that those goals would more effectively be attained by Jesus' manifestation through multiple bodies on the earth at the same time. In this is the fulfillment of the parable of the dragnet:

> *"Again, the kingdom of heaven is like a dragnet cast into the sea, and gathering fish of every kind; and when it was filled, they drew it up on the beach; and they sat down and gathered the good fish into containers, but the bad they threw away."* [22]

The fish caught in the net represent the people of the earth being drawn together into judgment. The intersecting points of the net represent true congregations of believers scattered around the globe bringing forth Jesus' manifestation in such a way that it draws all the earth into judgment. Right now we are somewhere between Jesus' ministry on the earth and His return. We may be able to see the signs of our times[23] and discern that we may well be drawing near to His coming, but in actuality none of us know the day or the hour.[24] We must be diligent, therefore, to have our oil supply up-to-date and to keep our lamps trimmed and burning,[25] that we might hasten the coming of His kingdom.[26]

---

[22] Matthew 13:37-48
[23] Matthew 24:32-33
[24] Matthew 24:36
[25] Matthew 25:1-13
[26] 2 Peter 3:11-12

Isaiah said (and Handel eloquently repeated in the beginning or his oratorio):

> *"The voice of him that crieth in the wilderness, prepare ye the way of the LORD, make straight in the desert a highway for our God."* [27]

Did that pertain to the coming of the Messiah two thousand years ago, or does it pertain to this age we are currently in as well? What did members of the first century churches do? How did they define their role? In the book of Acts we see the congregation of the church at Antioch

> *"... ministering to the Lord and fasting, the Holy Spirit said, 'Set apart for Me Barnabas and Saul for the work to which I have called them," when they had fasted and prayed and laid their hands on them, they sent them away."* [28]

What does it mean to "minister to the Lord?" How did they minister to Him? If they did such things, should we not also be doing likewise? Since they were not encumbered with two millennia of "church doctrine" did they have insight we no longer have? When Jesus said ..."*I am the way, and the truth, and the life; no one comes to the Father but through me"* [29] was He speaking (as surely we have all been taught) concerning final judgment, or was He giving us instruction for approaching the Father in worship? We will tackle these topics as we seek His desired way for us to approach the thrones. [30]

---

[27] Isaiah 40:3 (KJV)
[28] Acts 13:2-3
[29] John 14:6
[30] Revelation 20:4

The Map

The goal, therefore, is for all of us to fully understand this "body" phenomena and how it relates to our function in worship, both as individual members of a body and as a body. The goal is also for each of us to understand our place and purpose in His manifestation through us. Everyone, from accomplished professional musicians, to pastors, and even the most musically illiterate member will benefit greatly from reading this book. As with an athletic team, the strength or depth of worship that is achieved will be as strong or deep as the weakest player; that is the individual who understands the least about the body and our approach before the throne. This book is meant to be the map to help us individually and to help congregations (bodies) everywhere greatly advance in our depth of worship, which in turn will advance His coming kingdom as He is more boldly manifested through those bodies in the earth.

What is Worship?

Before even asking this question it is important to clarify the fact that praise and worship are not the same thing. Having been a public high school choral director, I have discussed this issue with literally hundreds of parents and students, and as an accomplished singer I have visited more churches than I can count, only to find that most do not know that there is even a difference between praise and worship. Webster tells us that praise is "the expression of approval, commendation." The word in English comes from the Latin *"pretiare"* meaning 'to prize.' "Praise" is a tool that good educators use consistently. In college education courses I was taught to "catch a child doing something good and praise him/her for it." Recognize that they are doing something correctly and let them know it is good and you appreciate their work. Terms such as "very good," "I'm impressed," and "that was awesome" we do not hesitate to pour out on children as we are encouraging their development. Statements of this nature that are spoken or sung to God constitute praise. As parents our children bring us drawings that are really scribbling, but we tell them how beautiful they are because we see that their heart's desire is to bring us something they made that is special. This is surely how God sees us when we come before Him, and why Jesus taught us about our heavenly Father who loves us.[31] Even if you cannot see that He has done anything recently in your life, He created all things and gave life to you. This alone is worthy of great praise.

Worship is a little more difficult to define. Webster also tells us that worship is "worthiness, repute, respect, reverence paid to a divine being." Honestly, that tells us almost nothing. That definition also works in a variety of "lifeless" settings, or for congregations that actually only accomplish praise. Worship is intimacy with God. It occurs when we are brought to such a posture of awe that our hearts are melted before Him. Body members often weep and may also drop to their knees or even to their faces as they prostrate themselves before Him. As members of a congregation we get to this posture through praise and humility. He then replaces our stony hearts with a heart of flesh.[32] In this setting we are open to His touch. We sense, feel, or know His very presence. He is free to work in us and speak to us. We are content to be right there before Him and have no desire to be anywhere else. This phenomenon should be a reality to all true believers, and yet it appears to be somewhat rare. In many cases pastors

---

[31] John 14:21-23; 16:27
[32] Ezekiel 11:19; 36:26

(ministers/priests) and music leaders (directors) avoid it at all cost, possibly because it is intensely vulnerable, which is scary, and it presents an uncontrollable environment (not uncontrollable to Jesus but to them).

If you have observed religious services for other religions (not just denominations of Christianity) you will find that most also use music in their services. The concept of unified expression is at least easily initiated through song. When people sing together the music itself gives them a dimension of unity. They say the same words at the same time, and at the same tempo (speed). If a song is well written it will magnify the text. In most cases the songwriter considers the text, and what it is the poet is attempting to say. Then as they write the music they say more with the music than the text is able to express. Consider this statement made by the apostle John:

> I saw another strong angel coming down out of heaven, clothed with a cloud; and the rainbow was upon his head, and his face was like the sun, and his feet like pillars of fire; and he had in his hand a little book which was open. He placed his right foot on the sea and his left on the land; and he cried out with a loud voice, as when a lion roars; and when he had cried out, the seven peals of thunder uttered their voices. When the seven peals of thunder had spoken, I was about to write; and I heard a voice from heaven saying, "Seal up the things which the seven peals of thunder have spoken and do not write them." [33]

Our first response to this text is that we probably want to know what the thunder said. Since we are not going to

---

[33] Revelation 10:1-4

know the answer to that question in this flesh, let us just consider the fact that the thunder actually spoke, which therefore raises the question, 'Does the thunder speak when we hear it in a thunder storm and we just don't understand what it is saying?' What other things around us may be speaking to us and we are unable to understand or discern what is being said? If the songwriter is writing "in the Spirit," does the music itself speak into our souls with meaning that extends beyond the text of the lyrics? Perhaps all music communicates in this way and is inspired by some "spirit" (not necessarily the Holy Spirit). Unfortunately some of the most easily identifiable examples of this are found in the counterfeit.

I have attended a few rock concerts in my time and been amazed by the worship that occurred. First, we were conditioned in our youth to know that these artists are "cool" and if you also really like their work you can be "cool" too. After paying high fees for concert tickets, people assemble by the tens of thousands in an arena or stadium for the performance. Most ingest some form of a mind-altering substance. The first concert I attended, I did not do that. Yet, as I sat waiting for the show to begin there was so much marijuana in the room that everyone got "high" just from being there. The music was immensely powerful. Most musicians know that there is a difference between loud and powerful. Loudness by itself can be just noise, but powerful is so strong that you can feel the music in your chest and bones. As we were leaving we encountered a group of deaf people who had attended the show. They were explaining to someone who knew how to "sign" that they were there because they could feel the music. The musicians on the stage were amazingly good at playing their instruments, so at the end of the evening I expected a standing ovation. I did not expect the whole arena to suddenly get so quiet you could hear a pin drop while everyone was holding up lit cigarette lighters. It immediately struck me that this was real worship and completely unlike anything I had known in my Protestant experience. But who was being worshiped? I assumed it was the musicians on the stage, but have since come to consider the spiritual principality that was presiding over the event. It was at best idolatry. The mind-altering drugs, to which concert goers voluntarily subjected themselves, not only made them feel good but also allowed individuals to give themselves over to a spirit that would unify them in worship. The apostle Paul encourages us to not be drunk with wine but to be drunk in the Holy Spirit.[34] This way we voluntarily give ourselves over to His Spirit so that we can be brought into a unity whereby we can worship the true and living God, Creator of all things.

Who Should Worship?

Our immediate response would be that everyone should worship God, and it is biblically founded. In Psalms we read:

> "Let heaven and earth praise Him, the seas and everything that moves in them." [35]

and

> "All the ends of the earth will remember and turn to the LORD, and all the families of the nations will worship before You." [36]

---

[34] Ephesians 5:18-20
[35] Psalm 69:34
[36] Psalm 22:37

King David identifies that everyone should praise and everyone should worship, but what makes people want to worship? People in general do not worship until they witness an undeniable miracle. On occasion you hear of a hurricane or tornado that destroys everything in its path for miles, but one house in the middle of it is practically untouched. It seems likely that the owner would drop to his/her knees and worship God (especially if they were in the house when it occurred). Anyone can do this at any time, but for the body member there is a fuller motive. It is important to note that there is a difference in how the peoples of the nations might worship God from that of members of a body.

What is Body Worship?

Let us consider this statement. *"For where two or three have gathered together in My name, I am there in their midst."* [37] Based on this verse, I once thought that if two or three of my Christian friends happened to meet with me in some unexpected location we could have "church." Sometimes important things are lost in translation. The word "gathered" in the Greek text is passive, which simply means that someone else did the gathering. Jesus is the one who assembles (at least) two or three people together in a geographic location so that He might be consistently manifested "in their midst." It is unquestionably clear to those individuals that He is the one who has assembled them and that this is their purpose and function. Based upon their personal revelation in Him, they desire with all their being to be the vehicle of His manifestation on the earth. How they worship affects those assembled with

---

[37] Matthew 18:20

them, and the potential can be both positive and negative. They must now be sensitive to the Lord and to the other members of the body. They now have the responsibility of presenting their worship in ways that both honor God and edify (build up) their brothers and sisters. The goal is that Jesus would be manifested through this assembled group and be free to do the same things He did as He walked this earth. There should be no limitation to what Jesus would be able to accomplish through the body He has assembled.

On the other hand Satan, who Jesus referred to as the ruler or *"prince of this world,"* [38] will do everything he can to stop or prevent Jesus' manifestation. Although he has other means, and uses them as well, his simplest tool for accomplishing this task is disunity. Members of the body invariably become close enough to see one another's differences, especially those differences that are undesirable. The apostle Paul exhorts us to know no one according to the flesh.[39] We must, therefore, see them as God sees them; that is, we must focus on their potentials and overlook their shortcomings, even as we hope our potentials are fulfilled and our shortcomings are over looked.

Where Did Things Go Wrong?

Without going deeply into church history, a few things musically are rather obvious. The apostle John wrote the last book of the bible, the first three chapters dealing with Jesus' correction to established churches. We would like to think they listened to His directives, and they probably did for a time, but it seems evident that the enemy was hard at work.

---

[38] John 14:30
[39] 2 Corinthians 5:16

The very early chants that are still heard from time to time in the Catholic Church are referred to as Gregorian chants. Gregory was not the person who wrote the chants, he was the Pope of the Roman Catholic Church (from 590-604) when some poor unknown monk decided they all needed to be written down or they would be lost. The chants, though written in Latin, sound amazingly similar to those who sing "in the Spirit," and they probably date back to very early, many of them possibly even to the first century. They are very free in form, usually lacking a defined beat and without any harmony. Soon harmony did develop though, as monks divided into high and low voices, and then boys were added (it was considered improper for women to sing in public well into the nineteenth century). By the Renaissance Period this developed into Motets, which are the religious form of a Madrigal. Both are highly complex compositional styles that are "polyphonic" in form, which means that there are usually four of five different melodies occurring at the same time. Although this may seem to be a harmlessly normal development musically, it is a disaster with regard to "the body." An unhealthy separation, even elitism had developed and was firmly established by this time (Renaissance period). It is a separation between those who are musically literate from those who, frankly, do not sing well. The problem is magnified by the development of the pipe organ. Although it is a magnificent instrument that can express awe and majesty, it is also an instrument that by the thirteenth century was easily able to drown out bad singers. There is a place for a quality presentation by a choir, a pianist or organist, a group of instrumentalists or dancers as an offering before the Lord. This, however, cannot replace the importance of every individual's ability to participate physically and vocally in the function of the body in worship and, therefore, the manifestation of Jesus. When the congregation is worshiping, it cannot matter if someone sounds bad. God is listening to their heart, not their voice.

Jesus makes a very important point that is often misunderstood and missed. In addressing the church at Ephesus through the apostle John He says,

> *"Yet this you do have, that you hate the deeds of the Nicolaitans, which I also hate."* [40]

Since many of the names of the cities in that area sound much alike, I always assumed that these "Nicolaitans" were the people of some town nearby. They are not. In Greek the word "Nicos" means to conquer. Who is being conquered? That would be the "laitans," or "laity." Jesus hates the works of the "conquerors of the laity" because they completely squelch any opportunity for His manifestation. In doing so, they as members of the body, have made themselves tools in the hand of Satan in stopping Jesus from being manifested through that congregation. Jesus hates the division of "clergy" and "laity," and He brought forth this warning probably around 70 A.D.

Today, in many churches electronic keyboards, electric guitars and a drum set, have replaced the pipe organ, but the end result is the same. If the music is too loud for the individual members to be heard, there is no opportunity for Jesus to be manifested. Notice that I did not say these instruments are the reason for the problem. It is the volume at which they are often played that conquers the body manifestation. If you cannot clearly hear the congregation singing, just turn the volume down!

---

[40] Revelation 2:6

2. God's Revelation: How He Wants To Be Approached

Just after "the fall" there immediately arose a problem between the two sons of Adam and Eve. Both brought an offering to the Lord. Cain was a farmer. His brother Abel was a "keeper of flocks." Logically then Abel brought a sacrificed animal to the Lord and Cain brought the produce of his farming.

> "And the LORD had regard for Abel and for his offering; but for Cain and for his offering He had no regard. So Cain became very angry and his countenance fell." [41]

It appears the Lord has favorites, or did Cain do something wrong? The scripture never comes out and tells us, but it seems evident that God had made it clear that the animal sacrifice was what He required. When Adam and Eve sinned, they realized their nakedness and covered themselves by sewing fig leaves together.[42] God later clothed them in animal skins.[43] Where did He get the animal skins? He must have shown them how to make an animal sacrifice for their sin and in the process established the acceptable pattern.

The Patriarchs

It is apparent that God reveals Himself to us more and more as we individually grow in Him and that His revelation

---

[41] Genesis 4:4b-5
[42] Genesis 3:7
[43] Genesis 3:21

to mankind also has increased consistently throughout the scriptures, so we might expect that Abraham's worship experience was comparably infantile. Although Abraham did not have a bible to read I would argue that his worship experience was real and very tangible. Abraham clearly initiated his worship experience with animal sacrifices. In our society few of us have ever had to butcher our own meat, so most of us really do not understand how a sacrifice can constitute worship. If asked to make a sacrifice we assume it is something that will moderately inconvenience us, or that we will have to go without something for a time. In Abraham's time, for any shepherd or herdsman the ability to feed their household was dependant on the reproduction and healthy growth of their livestock. Taking the best of the herd or flock, those who you would want to use for reproducing a hearty livestock, and just killing it was a real sacrifice and an act of faith. If famine later occurred, it could cost the lives of one's household.

Witnessing the death of any being is quite a stark reality. The recognition of the fact that sin causes the need for a substitute death is very humbling. Our worship experience does not require a sacrifice, but it does require the recognition of the ultimate sacrifice God has made on our behalf through Jesus. This is not just an important ingredient in our approach to God, but it is critical and foundational.

In Hebrew, the word קָרַב (pronounced KaRAV) means to approach, as in coming near or approaching the Throne of God. By adding one letter to that spelling a new word is identified - קָרְבָן (pronounced korBAN), meaning offering, sacrifice, or victim.[44] It is not difficult for us to see from this

---
[44] Leviticus 1:2

that the prescribed approach before the throne is through sacrifice.

Interestingly, Abram does not worship when the Lord first speaks to him and tells him to leave his country and his relatives and *"go to the land to which I will show you."* [45] After Abram arrived in the land (at Shechem) the Lord appeared to him. It does not expound on how the Lord appeared to him, but it was profound enough for Abram to build two altars in response to that appearance.[46] He surely built those altars for the purpose of making sacrifices, and thus worshiping. These are not sin sacrifices but would equate to a peace offering as later described in the book of Leviticus.[47]

After returning from Egypt Abram went back to the altar and *"called on the name of the Lord."* [48] After his difficulty with Lot and their subsequent separation, the Lord chose to show Abram all the land that He was giving him. Abram walked the length and breadth of it. He then moved far to the south and established his household near Hebron and built another altar there, having received that profound revelation.[49] Since he quickly built an altar near his new residence, it seems apparent that Abram wanted to be prepared to worship regularly. God also required Abram to make a blood sacrifice to seal His covenant (contract) with Abram and his descendants. He gave them the land situated between the river of Egypt and the Euphrates River *forever.*[50]

---

[45] Genesis 12:1
[46] Genesis 12:7-8
[47] Leviticus: chapters 1-5
[48] Genesis 13:4
[49] Genesis 13:18
[50] Genesis 15:18

It is important to see that God did not commune with Abram for a time. Hagar was evidently one of the gifts Pharaoh gave Abram,[51] and since Sarah was not conceiving she gave Hagar to Abram as a concubine.[52] God apparently did not appreciate Abram's vacillation of faith, or his feeling the need to help God fulfill His promise. When Ishmael was born Abram was eighty-six years old.[53] The next interaction Abram had with the Lord was when he was ninety-nine, at which point *"Abram fell on his face, and God talked with Him"*[54] and made great promises to him, and even gave him his new name. Notice here the intimacy of their relationship and the absence of religious trappings.

The next time Abraham built an altar it meant revelation for Isaac as well. Apparently, it was a result of a *land-for-peace* deal Abraham made with Abimelech, the Philistine King,[55] possibly in an effort to protect Isaac's future in the land. God tested Abraham's faith by telling him to

> *"Take now your son, your only son, whom you love, Isaac, and go to the land of Moriah, and offer him there as a burnt offering on one of the mountains of which I will tell you."*[56]

Isaac was not Abraham's only son, but in the eyes of God he was. Isaac was the heir of Abraham's inheritance and the one through which the promises of God would be fulfilled.[57] The writer of the book of Hebrews tells us that

---

[51] Genesis 12:16
[52] Genesis 16:1-4
[53] Genesis 16:16
[54] Genesis 17:1-4
[55] Genesis 21:22-34
[56] Genesis 22:2
[57] Genesis 17:19

Abraham must have considered God's ability to raise someone from the dead in order that he might fulfill His promises.[58] Isaac surely understood what was happening as his father bound his hands and feet. He may have heard an audible voice from heaven but even if he did not, he knew something stopped his father from killing him. Abraham did sacrifice the ram caught in the thicket[59] and you can be sure Isaac was praising and worshiping along with his father.

Isaac later built an altar of his own at Beersheba and called upon the name of the Lord. Like his father Abraham, this again was after the Lord appeared to him and confirmed through him the promises He had made to Abraham.[60]

Jacob had a great dream. In it he saw a ladder reaching into heaven with angels moving up and down on it. The Lord was at the top of the ladder and He confirmed the same promises He had previously made to Jacob's father and grandfather. He also promised to bring Jacob back to the land. When Jacob awoke he was awestruck with reality and declared, *"How awesome is this place!"*[61] He renamed that location "the house of God" (Bethel) and "the gate of heaven."[62] He also erected a commemorative pillar, but he did not build an altar, probably because he was fleeing from his brother and wanted to "get out of town" as fast as he could.

Twenty years later he returned and heard that his brother Esau, who had previously vowed to kill Jacob, was coming

---

[58] Hebrews 11:17-19
[59] Genesis 22:9-12
[60] Genesis 26:23-25
[61] Genesis 28:17
[62] Genesis 28:17-19

out to meet him with a small army.[63] Petrified, Jacob wrestled all night "with a man" [64] who apparently was much more than just a man, since He had the authority to change Jacob's name to "Israel." Finally, broken before the Lord, he came to his brother, bowing before him and humbly 'bearing his neck.' [65] They embrace and rejoiced, and both returned to the land.[66] When Jacob settled in at Shechem he finally built an altar, and called it El-Elohe-Israel,[67] which means "God, the God of Israel," implying not just his God, but the God of his descendants who would be named Israel as a nation.

Interestingly, not long after Jacob had returned to the land God instructed him not only to go back to Bethel, but also to move there and build an altar where the Lord had first met him, which he obediently did.[68]

The Nation of Israel

Some four hundred years later Israel had been incubated into a substantial nation while enslaved in Egypt. God raised up Moses to lead His people out of Egypt and back into the land consistently promised to all three of the Patriarchs and their descendants forever. Although Moses had a bold revelation experience (at the burning bush), as did the Patriarchs, the focus had now moved to the nation of Israel with Moses as their special servant. After Israel exited Egypt, God led them to Mount Sinai where the people witnessed fearful manifestations of the physical

---

[63] Genesis 32:6
[64] Genesis 32:24
[65] Genesis 33:3
[66] Genesis 33:13-14
[67] Genesis 33:20
[68] Genesis 35:1-7

presence of God.[69] Moses went up onto the mountain, stood directly in His presence and in the process was shown amazing things. Specifically, he was shown the layout of the throne room in heaven and instructed to build a replica in physical terms on the earth.[70] God instructed them to build a tabernacle in the middle of the camp of Israel, which is in the middle of the nations of the earth.

The Tabernacle

The word "sanctuary" is often used to describe the tabernacle, but it falls somewhat short of the full picture. It is easy to see that the word "sanctuary" is a derivative of the Latin word "sanctus," which means "holy, sanctified or set apart," thus implying that it is the "Holy Place." The term used in the original Hebrew text is "Mikdosh."

> "Let them construct a sanctuary (מִקְדָּשׁ - Mikdosh) for Me, that I may dwell (שָׁכַן - shaKHAN) among them."[71]

"Shakhan" means to lodge, settle down, abide, or dwell. From this statement we can see that God's intention is for the "Mikdosh" to actually be "God's Holy Residence" in the earth.

Very near the end of the book of Revelation the apostle John tells us:

---

[69] Exodus 19:16-19; 20:18-21
[70] Exodus 25:9; 25:40; 26:30; 27:8
[71] Exodus 25:8

"And I heard a loud voice from the throne, saying, 'Behold, the tabernacle of God is among men, and He will dwell among them, and they shall be His people, and God Himself will be among them...'" [72]

As soon as Israel is established as the wife of God,[73] He openly expresses His desire to dwell right in the middle of their community. It is, has been and always will be the desire of God's heart to dwell in the midst of His people. With that in mind let us look closer at the layout of the tabernacle.

It has two rooms divided by a curtain. The first room is called the "holy place." It contains a seven-branch lamp stand or "menorah" (representing the light of the world), a table for the bread of Presence (representing the bread of life), and a table of incense (representing the fact that we have "one mediator-between God and men, the man Christ [Messiah] Jesus)." [74] As Christians we understand this room to represent Jesus. The second room is called the "Most Holy Place" or the "Holy of Holies," and it, therefore, represents the Father. It is where the Ark of the Covenant was located.

The Ark is a small wooden box or trunk, about the size of a piano bench, and completely overlaid with pure gold. Its lid has two "cherubim" (usually described in the bible as lion looking creatures with two wings) seated on the top facing each other with their heads lowered and their wings stretched out toward each other. The lid is called the mercy seat and constitutes the very throne of the glory of God on the earth.[75] When it was completed, along with the taber-

---

[72] Revelation 21:3
[73] Exodus 19:5-8
[74] 1 Timothy 2:5
[75] Exodus 25

nacle and its' other furnishings, the presence of God was physically manifested in the earth between its wings.[76] The second set of the Ten Commandments written on the two tablets of stone by the hand of God was placed inside the ark.[77] Two other objects that, at least for a time, had been placed in the ark were the rod of Aaron and a jar of the "manna" from the wilderness.[78] Notice that His throne is called the mercy seat (for which we are all grateful), but that it is seated on His law, or definition of right and wrong.

An outer court was erected around the tent with a larger area in front. It contained an altar for fire and a water laver. If a person sinned they brought their offering to the gate of the outer court where a priest met them. From there the

---

[76] Exodus 25:22; 40:34-35; Numbers 7:89
[77] Deuteronomy 10:1-5
[78] Hebrews 9:4

priest would make the sacrifice on the altar. The individual sinner was not permitted into the outer court. If a priest was to minister in the Holy Place, after making a sacrifice he would wash in the water laver. From there he could then enter into the holy place and attend to the items in that room, as did Zacharias, the father of John the Baptist.[79] Passing through the curtain into the Most Holy Place was reserved for one priest one day out of the year, the Day of Atonement (Yom Kippur).[80]

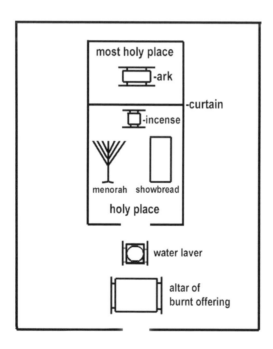

For us, when we realized our sin, we accepted the sacrifice made on our behalf represented by the brazen altar. It was

---

[79] Luke 1:5-12
[80] Leviticus 16:29-34

then our responsibility to study the scriptures and wash out the doctrinal teachings with which many of us were raised, represented by the water laver.[81] Then we are free to enter into the presence of Him who is the bread of life, the light of the world, our mediator who, by the blood of His sacrifice has made the two separate rooms into one and, therefore, ushers us before His Father.[82] This is nothing less than awesome and constitutes an amazingly clear picture of approach before the throne of God. Although music is not presented as a part of this prescribed approach, we will later discuss its function and importance in this process.

The Levites

Levi was one of the sons of Jacob (Israel), therefore, Levi's offspring are referred to as the Levites. In a round about way they were selected to be the priests of Israel. God's initial plan was that the first-born male of each household would be one of the priests,[83] but later decided it should be the Levites.[84] As priests they were called upon to *intercede*[85] on behalf of all of Israel and served specific functions in fulfilling that role. Notice that this radically differs from the "clergy" perspective prevalent in modern denominational churches. The Levites were dedicated to maintaining the tabernacle and it's furnishings, and the "Cohenim" (a special group of Levites) were also responsible for making the sacrifices.

---

[81] Romans 12:2; Ephesians 4:22-24; 5:26
[82] Luke 23:45; Hebrews 10:19-22
[83] Exodus 13:2; Numbers 3:13
[84] Numbers 3:45-49; Deuteronomy 10:6-9
[85] Numbers 21:7; Isaiah 53:12

The Sacrifices

God identified five specific types of sacrifices presenting a fuller perspective of how we should approach Him. He began with the burnt offering, which is the one closest to Him. We actually have to look at them in the reverse order and begin with the one closest to us.

The guilt offering is our first step in getting close to God. These violations often constitute touching unclean things, but also include swearing thoughtlessly (making an oath). It may have been a violation of some sort that was previously unseen, but now has been revealed. All constitute sin and the individual perpetrator would have to bring a specified offering to the tabernacle where the priest would sacrifice it and make atonement before the Lord on their behalf.[86] The sin offering is our second step and it is similar to the guilt offering in that a specified sacrifice is made in a specific manner.[87]

The third is the peace offering and it is notably different from the previous two. An animal that is without defect is still sacrificed and the blood is still sprinkled on the altar. In this case, however, the individual bringing the sacrifice is confident in the previous two sacrifices and is now simply interested in being at peace with God.[88]

The fourth confusingly goes by many names based on which translation of the bible you are reading. The gift (grain, meat, cereal, meal) offering is often referred to as a service offering. It could be offered in many forms all of which were made from unleavened fine flour mixed with

---

[86] Leviticus 5
[87] Leviticus 4
[88] Leviticus 3

oil.[89] Finally the fifth is the burnt offering, where the defined sacrifice is completely consumed (burned to ashes) on the altar.[90]

It is not difficult to see that each of these sacrifices represents a stage or level of understanding in the life of the believer. When we realize we have been heading down the wrong path we repent, or turn away from that path (or behavior). We recognize we have been guilty of offensives (guilt offering) and we are totally incapable of fixing the problem. With great appreciation we recognize the sacrifice that was made on our behalf, and determine to *"go and sin no more"* [91] (sin offering). We also deal with seemingly lesser issues of attitudes and motives. We come to a position of peace with God (peace offering). We determine that there are actually things we can do to serve God, minister to God, and even advance His coming kingdom, and we choose to serve Him and His body with a willing heart (gift offering). Finally, we become completely consumed in our desire for Him and His kingdom (burnt offering). This pattern is for every individual, and is a necessary walk in the life of every body member.

King David

King David presents a very unique model that is extremely important for us to see. David's life presents a unique aspect of the role and function of (for him) the coming Messiah. There are a few people in the Hebrew Scriptures that are "Messiah" types. Isaac, being brought by his father to Mount Moriah (later called Mount Zion) where his father

---

[89] Leviticus 2
[90] Leviticus 1
[91] John 8:11c

was to sacrifice his only son, is clearly one. Another is Joseph, beginning from humble means, but then established by Pharaoh (the king or emperor) as ruler over his entire kingdom (as Jesus has been placed in authority over everything).[92] A third who is also quite obvious is Moses as he functioned in the three capacities of prophet, priest and king. King David, like Moses, also functioned as prophet, priest and king, but there is much more. To fully understand this concept we will consider specific events in David's life.

Although David was a heroic individual in the scriptures, he was also human and, therefore, made a few errors. One big mistake cost the life of his servant Uzzah. Prior to the time of David's predecessor, King Saul, while Israel was functioning under the judgeship of Eli, the army of Israel was losing a war against the Philistines. The elders of Israel sent for the Ark to be brought to the battlefield, but the Ark is not to be treated like a good luck charm. They lost the battle, and with it, the Ark[93] was taken to a Philistine city called Ashdod. The Philistines did not know what to do with it, so they put it in the house of their god, Dagon (a half-fish half-man idol). The next morning they found Dagon face down in the dirt before the Ark of the God of Israel. They set Dagon back up on his pedestal, but found him the next morning again in the dirt with his head and arms cut off.[94] Then God smote the people of Ashdod with tumors, or hemorrhoids. From a modern medical perspective, mice that were following the ark were carrying dysentery, causing diarrhea, bleeding hemorrhoids, and death.[95] The Philistines moved it from Ashdod to Gaza, then to Ashkelon, Gath and finally Ekron before they decided they

---

[92] Ephesians 1:20-23; 1 Corinthians 15:27-28
[93] 1 Samuel 4
[94] 1 Samuel 5:4
[95] 1 Samuel 6:5

had enough. They placed the ark on a new cart (with an offering of five gold hemorrhoids and five gold mice, one for each city) drawn by two cows that were still nursing their calves. They determined that if the cows carried the Ark to Israel rather than returning to their hungry calves, the God of Israel had caused their distress and was taking the Ark back to the Israelis, which is how it happened.[96] Unfortunately, some of the people of the first Israeli town to which it came were foolish and they opened the Ark and took a look inside. The Lord struck them with a great slaughter for doing so. The Ark was moved to Kiriath-jearim and stayed there for twenty years.[97] In the meantime King Saul was killed in battle.

David ruled as king over Hebron seven years and six months. Then the heads of the tribes of Israel came to David and anointed him to be king over all of Israel. David could have gone after many battlefronts, but his first action was to go up against the Jebusites and take Jerusalem.[98] He then took thirty thousand men with him and went to Kiriath-jearim to bring the Ark to himself in Jerusalem. They took a new cart drawn by oxen and put the Ark on it (as the Philistines had done) and set off for Jerusalem. The oxen nearly upset the cart, so Uzzah reached out and grabbed the Ark to steady it, but the Lord struck him down for his irreverence and he died.

The event caused David to research the scriptures to see what he had done wrong. Then he said:

> *"No one is to **carry** the ark of God but the Levites; for the LORD chose them to **carry** the ark of God and to minister to Him forever."* [99]

---

[96] 1 Samuel 6:7-12
[97] 1 Samuel 7
[98] 2 Samuel 5:1-9
[99] 1 Chronicles 15:1

David understood that if God had a prescribed way of doing something, he needed to do it His way. Here is what David must have read.

> "You shall put the poles into the rings on the sides of the ark, to **carry** the ark with them." [100]

> "At that time the LORD set apart the tribe of Levi to **carry** the ark of the covenant of the LORD, to stand before the LORD to serve Him and to bless in His name until this day." [101]

Although this cleared up the issue of how the ark should be transported, more happens here than first meets the eye. It seems evident that Samuel had moved the tabernacle that Moses had built from Shiloh (some twenty miles north of Jerusalem) to Gibeon.[102] Those who have toured Israel and visited Samuel's tomb have been to Gibeon. From there you can see Jerusalem without straining. David must have had a clear word from the Lord that he should bring the Ark into Jerusalem, and not simply take it "off just a little to the left" and put it in the most likely place for it, the place where it was designed to go, the tabernacle built by Moses currently located in Gibeon. Uzzah's death must have caused David to question if he had heard correctly from the Lord. When he set out to move the Ark again, he made sacrifices every six steps they took.[103] They brought it into Jerusalem with loud, abandoned praise; dancing, shouting and the sound of the trumpets, and David put it in another tent that he had prepared for it![104]

---

[100] Exodus 25:14
[101] Deuteronomy 10:8
[102] 1 Chronicles 21:29; 2 Chronicles 1:3-4
[103] 2 Samuel 6:13
[104] 2 Samuel 6:17

There are two tents (tabernacles)! We have to assume that there is no dividing curtain in David's tent (separating the Holy Place from the Most Holy Place) since all the other furniture is not mentioned in the move. Those things, therefore, must have remained in the tabernacle at Gibeon. It also seems evident that not only King David, but also all the Levites, and virtually all the people of Israel were able to walk in and out of the tent before the Ark of God and not die. The drawings below demonstrate how things would have been handled differently between the two tents.

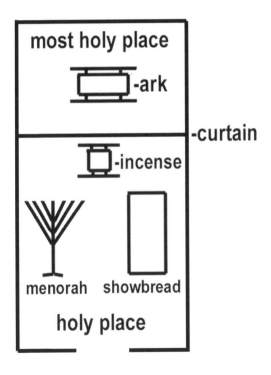

Tabernacle built by Moses - interior

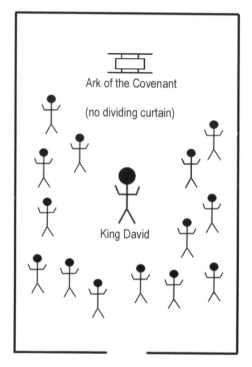

Ark of the Covenant

(no dividing curtain)

King David

Tabernacle built by King David - interior

After King David's death his son Solomon built the stone temple, along with new furnishings, and everything returned to how it was before David. What this then implies, is that during his life, King David was meant to be such a strong picture of the Messiah to come that he even functioned as the mediator for the people of Israel before God. For this reason we must take a closer look at this thing we call Davidic worship.

Davidic Praise and Worship

Many think for it to be "Davidic" praise the music has to be "Hebraic," with a Yemenite rhythm, or at least in a minor key. Others express that you have to be able to dance in a Hebraic style or wear Hebraic costumes, and on and on. All of these scream of an identity crisis, but they bear no relevance to the heart condition. Davidic praise is a free, abandoned, genuine, truthful appreciation of God's abounding love, forgiveness, and faithfulness. It can be Hebraic in nature, but that is not necessary.

Davidic worship is a free and uninhibited expression before the Lord. By its very nature it is highly vulnerable to abuse. There seems to unfortunately always be those who draw attention to themselves. They wear a "look at me" spirit that is repulsive to everyone who sees it. They seem to think that no one can see their motive when in reality it is highly recognized by most of the congregation. That attitude purposely draws attention away from the Lord and on to that individual. Davidic worship (as king David's life demonstrated) is a genuine desire for a heart-to-heart, face-to-face intimacy with God. The selected music must be tender and intimate love songs. If you would not shout a love song into the face of your mate, then surely you should not do likewise to the Lord. Shouting or singing boisterously is appropriate for praise, but in worship we are seeking tender intimacy. The tempo (speed of the beat) should be very free, and somewhat "rubato" in style. It is often very difficult when working with many musicians to express this freedom and so it may be appropriate for some to stop playing, join with the congregation in singing, and let that one guitar or piano/keyboard present the song by itself. Awkward as it may be, worship leaders need to tactfully exercise authority (under the authority of the pastor) and insist on those things that enable true worship to occur.

24/7

Another unique attribute to worship during the reign of King David is not clearly stated but can be safely assumed. David split the two hundred eighty eight skillful musicians he had into twenty-four groups of twelve. They then ministered (in groups of twelve) in the tent before the Ark of God (i.e. His very presence) on a rotating schedule, for they had *"cast lots for their duties."* [105] Since they did not have wristwatches or clocks, we cannot say that a relief crew came in "every hour on the hour," but somehow throughout the week those twenty-four groups kept praise and worship happening (ministering) before the Throne of God continually.

Song of Songs

After the temple of stone was built (following the death of King David)[106] everything returned to how it had previously been done in the tabernacle, but some things could never again be as they were. King Solomon (King David's second son by Bathsheba and successor to the throne) wrote three books of the bible. The most important to our purposes was named Song of Songs (Song of Solomon). It speaks boldly of the relationship between a man and a woman, and the expression is frankly embarrassingly intimate. Having the baffling knowledge that this Solomon, biblically deemed the wisest man who ever lived,[107] strayed from his walk in the Lord,[108] I always figured he was "on his way out" as he penned this seemingly lusty text.

---

[105] 1 Chronicles 25:8
[106] 1 Chronicles 28:3-5
[107] 2 Chronicles 1:9-12
[108] 1 Kings 11:6-10

I later learned that this work was and still is sung every year on the Sabbath that falls within the week of the eight-day Feast of Unleavened Bread (beginning with Passover on the fourteenth day of the first month on the Hebrew calendar).[109] Participants understood that although this text is a dialogue between a man, a woman, and a chorus (the daughters of Jerusalem), it is a reflection of God's desire for intimacy with his wife, Israel,[110] and therefore also His wife's desire for intimacy with Him. The same analogy can be drawn between the true church and Jesus, especially when we see the expressions "bride" and "bridegroom" being used to convey the consummated relationship at His coming.[111] It seems evident that these Israelis understood considerably more about worship than many of us may have considered, and at the very least a strong foundation was established.

Revelation in Jesus

Of the four gospel writers, I reference Luke first and absolutely the most. This is not only because Luke wrote more than the other three, but also because, not being a Jew, he tells us what happened in more detail, and he does not assume we already know all the customs and practices. When it comes to praise and worship though, they all seem to fall short. Luke does give us Jesus' response after the return of the seventy disciples He had sent out.

> *The seventy returned with joy, saying, "Lord, even the demons are subject to us in Your name." And He said to them, "I was watching Satan fall from heaven*

---

[109] Wikipedia.org
[110] Exodus 19
[111] Revelation 19:7-9

*like lightning. Behold, I have given you authority to tread on serpents and scorpions, and over all the power of the enemy, and nothing will injure you. Nevertheless do not rejoice in this, that the spirits are subject to you, but rejoice that your names are recorded in heaven." At that very time **He rejoiced greatly in the Holy Spirit**, and said, "I praise You, O Father, Lord of heaven and earth, that You have hidden these things from the wise and intelligent and have revealed them to infants. Yes, Father, for this way was well pleasing in Your sight. All things have been handed over to Me by My Father, and no one knows who the Son is except the Father, and who the Father is except the Son, and anyone to whom the Son wills to reveal Him."* [112]

As wonderful as this is, we never hear of any of them having any musical instruments or exercising any structured expression in praise and worship. The scripture does not identify a musician in the twelve, or even the seventy. It does reveal that they went to the temple in Jerusalem and synagogues throughout the region of Galilee.[113] Any praise and worship expressed in those places would have maintained the established religious liturgies. As I stated previously, Jesus himself introduced the concept of a body manifestation,[114] but it was after Jesus' ascension that we are able to see the concept of a body developing in the understanding of His disciples. At the newly established church at Antioch we see:

---

[112] Luke 10:17-22
[113] Luke 4:44
[114] John 2:19-21; Matthew 18:20

43

> *And while they were **ministering to the Lord** and fasting, the Holy Spirit said, "Set apart for me Barnabas and Saul for the work which I have called them."* [115]

As previously stated, what is meant by that term *"ministering to the Lord?"* We see it also in the Hebrew Scriptures:

> *"Now Samuel was **ministering before the Lord**, as a boy wearing a linen ephod."* [116]

The ephod is something that is worn by a priest; one who serves God and the people. Samuel rose up to be one of Israel's great prophets, and being a prophet requires hearing from God, and that requires intimacy with God. The term "ministering" brings out a very important perspective. Ministering to or before the Lord means that what we are doing is for Him, not for us. It is true that when we worship we receive His acceptance and the overwhelming knowledge of His love and forgiveness. Our reason for initiating worship however, cannot be self-oriented; it's not for us, it's for Him. In a right marriage relationship (a reflection of our relationship with God) partners understand the importance of giving. When both are focused on giving (ministering) to each other, the intimacy shared is greatly magnified. When one gives deeply and from the heart they also receive deeply, not giving to receive but simply giving out of pure love (not expecting something in return). Can you out-give God? If your giving to Him is with a pure motive will He not respond by giving in even greater measures? He alone is truly worthy! In worship each individual member must say, "No matter how I feel and even if things are not going my way, He is still worthy, and how I feel at the moment is frankly irrelevant." This is not

---

[115] Acts 13:2
[116] 1 Samuel 2:18

a hard-hearted perspective, it's a realistic perspective and God loves for us to embrace reality.

Notice that the congregation at Antioch was ministering and fasting corporately (united or combined into one). This is critical. The apostle Paul painstakingly describes the body in detail[117] with the intent for us to understand that it is the desire of Jesus that we function as one body, His body, with Jesus as the head of that body.

> *"Of this church I was made a minister according to the stewardship from God bestowed on me for your benefit, so that I might fully carry out the preaching of the word of God, that is, the mystery which has been hidden from the past ages and generations, but has now been manifested to His saints, to whom God willed to make known what is the riches of the glory of this mystery among the Gentiles, which is Christ in you, the hope of glory."* [118]

Paul's terminology is somewhat ambiguous, so allow me clarify this statement. First, the word "you" in the last verse is suffering from a deficiency of the English language, there is no plural word for "you." Different areas of the United States try to make up for this problem. Those who live in the south say "y'all," in the northeast – "yous guys," and in areas of the Midwest – "you'ins." The point is, Paul is saying that this mystery that has been hidden from everyone in the past has been made real in us, and it is Jesus manifested through His body (an assembly of believers) that is the hope of glory. His hope is not in any of us individually, but in a body of believers collectively with Jesus as the head.

---

[117] 1 Corinthians 12 & 14
[118] Colossians 1:25-27

I Am the Way

We know that sometimes finding those real nuggets of truth requires diligent study of the scriptures. If we couple that with the reality of nearly two thousand years of clouding church doctrine, some things are difficult to see, but by the grace of God they are not impossible to find. Let's look closely at this scripture:

> *"In My Father's house are many dwelling places; if it were not so, I would have told you; for I go to prepare a place for you. If I go and prepare a place for you, I will come again and receive you to Myself, that where I am, there you may be also. And you know the way where I am going. Thomas said to Him, 'Lord, we do not know where You are going, how do we know the way?' Jesus said to him, 'I am the way, and the truth, and the life; no one comes to the Father but through Me.'"* [119]

Surely we have all heard that last verse hundreds of times, but it is always taken out of context. Notice a couple of verses earlier Jesus said, *"And you know the way where I am going."* We all probably gave agreement with Thomas when he went on to say *'we don't know where you are going, how do we know the way?'* Jesus' direction, however, is not physical but spiritual. If He told them they already knew the way, then He had already taken them there before, in worship! He was giving directions to all of us as to how we can approach the Father right now as we walk the earth in this life. You can sit in a circle and hum, but that won't get you there. You can go to a medium and you may make contact with some kind of spiritual being (a deceiving spirit) but that won't get you to God. Jesus is the

---

[119] John 14:2-6

way, right here, right now, for us to enter into the throne room of the Creator of all things. Through Him we are able to reconnect in some measure what was lost when Adam and Eve rebelled. Just as we saw earlier in the model of the Mikdosh, we can enter the Most Holy Place (presence of the Father), but only through the Holy Place (the room containing the Menorah, Table of Showbread, and the Table of Incense) representing Jesus. By Jesus' sacrifice, the dividing curtain was torn from top to bottom and the two rooms are now made one.[120] Basking in His presence as we worship, we experience deliverance, healing, acceptance, peace, unconditional love and forgiveness. We are also then in a position for the King in our midst to be manifested through us, freely accomplishing His desires through us. It seems apparent that the first century church fully understood and functioned in this capacity. As shown in the following graphics, just as King David stood in the midst of the Levites, Jesus stands in the midst of His church. As David led those inside the tent in praise and worship before the Ark and, therefore, the very presence of God, so also and much more fully, Jesus himself leads those He has chosen in praise and worship before the throne of God.

---

[120] Matthew 27:51

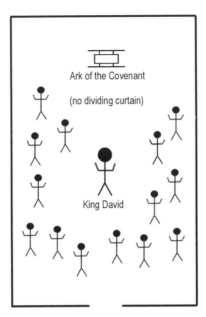

Tabernacle built by King David - interior

function of a true church

3. A Working Outline for Praise and Worship

From this section we have developed an outline that we use as we select songs for praise and worship. It is merely an outline, and since the real Jesus (son of the God of Abraham, Isaac and Jacob) is Lord in the midst of us, He is free to come in and change it at any time. I have come to find that He does like this outline though, and so we at least start out with it, and He usually continues it. It is very important for every individual of the congregation to understand the goal of each section. Jesus has called each member to be a part of this phenomenon, and, therefore, each one is crucial to it.

We begin with **Robust – Up-tempo Praise**. We all enter the building carrying cares and concerns. Our focus is usually not on the Lord but on our ornery children or the one who cut us off as we were driving to the church. We look to Jesus freeing us from those concerns as we praise. This section is where we can become "free" in the Spirit.[121] Without getting free we will have great difficulty going on, and continuing will be, at best, strained. Congregation members must understand their importance in the functioning of Jesus' body. If someone is not in attendance or simply does not feel like participating, that part of the body does not function, and that cripples Jesus' body. Everything we can do should be done to get free. Singing and hand clapping are a start, but members must be free to dance or jump; even do cart wheels or all kinds of acrobatics in joyous praise, like King David did as he brought the Ark into Jerusalem. As long as it encourages the congregation and does not draw attention to itself, it is good. If

---

[121] Ephesians 5:18

members want to do these things but are apprehensive about it, they can go to the back of the room and not risk inappropriate attention. I know that for many, this seems wild and crazy, but when we go to football games the band plays music, people sing and shout, cheerleaders dance and do all kinds of acrobatics, and all for twenty-two guys chasing a ball up and down the field. I, personally, really enjoy a good football game, but in the end, who won or lost the game will not stand before the throne of the Lord. In the end, what the Lord has done will stand forever. Whatever is good for a football game (or any other sport) is the least we can do for the Lord. Get over your hang-ups and give the Lord His praise.

We generally sing four to six songs in this category and connect them together into a "pseudo-medley" so that they build in tempo and intensity. For those who are playing musical instruments, the goal is to be the little engine that starts the big engine. The trained musicians who lead are not to do it all for the congregation, but to encourage and assist the whole congregation in participation.

We then pause to **Humble** ourselves. A big problem I have with popular Christian music is the fact that there are very few songs written for this category. It is critical that we consider and confess the reality of our fallen human condition and our need for the life of Jesus to be working in us continually. We generally sing only one piece in this category.

It is also critical that we confess our need for our brothers and sisters in the congregation. The phenomena we are pursuing is not possible without them, which brings us to our next interest, **Body Unity**. Often the people in the congregation are not necessarily the people with which we would choose to socialize. We have to recognize this fact, that is not why we are there, and that is not why they are there. These people are those whom Jesus has assembled together with us, for the purpose of bringing about His manifestation in the midst of us and in the geographic location where He placed us. Without them "standing"[122] with us, it does not happen. They are very important to us and they are probably even more important to Him. This is why gossip is so destructive. We must be very careful how we treat the chosen of the Lord. When Jesus appeared to Saul on the road to Damascus, He said, *"Saul, Saul; why are you persecuting Me."* [123] Jesus took Saul's actions against His elect very seriously and defined it as persecution against Himself. It is appropriate for the congregation to hold hands, hug, and speak blessings, to support and edify one another. We also generally sing only one song in this category.

Praise and Worship to Jesus follows "body unity." Now we look specifically for Jesus to enter in and take His headship in the midst of us. The text of the songs is critical. That means that if we use songs written by other composers, we often have to change the text. Most songs talk about Jesus, or the Father, or both – even at the same time. We want to speak **to** them and not **about** them. We want to clearly identify to whom we are speaking. Many modern Christian songs assume that if we are speaking to one we are speaking to all, which is not true. Here is why. When Jesus was questioned about marriage he quoted Genesis:

> *"Therefore shall a man leave his father and his mother, and shall cleave unto his wife: and they shall be one flesh."* [124]

---

[122] Ephesians 6:11-18
[123] Acts 22:7
[124] Genesis 2:24

The Hebrew word "one" in this case is plural. In English, we use similar terms, such as a "pair of shoes" or a "bunch of grapes." When a man and woman marry and "become one flesh" they do not loose their individual identities, but gain a unified identity with each other. They choose to minimize their individual identities for their collective identity, but they remain two individuals. Otherwise, to whom did/does Jesus pray?[125] Moses uses the same plural "one" when he said: *"Hear, O Israel! The LORD is our God, the LORD is one!"* [126] They remain individual identities and should not be confused with each other.

We usually do four to six songs in this section. We look to build to a hearty climax that is followed by an afterglow of intense and breathtaking intimacy. During this section the congregation should be able to discern "the King in the midst of the camp." It is appropriate for members to stand, kneel, and/or prostrate themselves. They should be free to do so anywhere in the room as long as they are not drawing attention onto themselves or causing any other member to not be able to worship. It is important to recognize that although we all want to be "lost in the moment" during this time, the *"the Spirits of prophets are subject to prophets; for God is not a God of confusion but of peace."* [127] What this means is that a member of the body may hear a word from the Lord, but it may not be for everyone. It may be just for that person. It is the responsibility of the individual to consider the word received and if it is for themselves or everyone. If they determine that it is for everyone, there is also an appropriate time to bring it forth, *"for God is not a God of confusion but of peace."* If the unified body is focused on Jesus and Harry starts

---

[125] Romans 8:34; Hebrews 7:24-25
[126] Deuteronomy 6:4
[127] 1 Corinthians 14:32-33a

praying for Aunt Jane, the focus is torn from Jesus. There is an appropriate time to pray for Aunt Jane, and it is Harry's job to bring it up in the right place. Likewise, if Harry has difficulty discerning when it is appropriate to intercede for Aunt Jane, it is also the job of the elders of the congregation to speak to Harry (if possible privately) to encourage him to edify the body and not focus on his family problems alone.

Members of the congregation must also be aware of an established momentum leading to a specific goal. When we were children we all learned about momentum as we learned to ride a bicycle, or later drive a car. As a high school choral director, I became acutely aware of a momentum in the classroom. I would purposely plan a class with activities that would lead my students toward a goal of unified quality singing. I knew I had achieved that goal when the class had ended and students were singing the recently rehearsed music as they exited the classroom. Phone or intercom interruptions or just some student asking to go to the restroom at the wrong time could be devastating to that momentum. Recovery during that session was often impossible. Members of the congregation must understand the importance of the momentum. If someone feels that they must deliver a word from God, they must also wait for the right time. If it will be substantially long, it probably should be brought forth after the worship time has ended. The most important thing that happens in an assembly is worship. Absolutely nothing should obstruct or even impede the congregation's ability to achieve deep and tender intimacy.

It is not appropriate in this, or any section, for anyone to howl at the moon, growl like a bear or bark like a dog. Of the nine gifts of the Holy Spirit absolutely none of them allude to any such manifestations. These are considerably more consistent with the manifestation of unholy spirits.

If "the King is in the camp" this section will give way to **Praise and Worship to the Father**. As we do this, we are actually living the fulfillment of Jesus' petition to the Father before going to the cross:

> *"I do not ask You to take them out of the world, but to keep them from the evil one. They are not of the world, even as I am not of the world. Sanctify them in the truth; Your word is truth. As You sent Me into the world, I also have sent them into the world. For their sakes I sanctify Myself, that they themselves also may be sanctified in truth.* **I do not ask on behalf of these alone, but for those also who believe in Me through their word; that they may all be one; even as You, Father, are in Me and I in You, that they also may be in Us, so that the world may believe that You sent Me.***"* [128]

Here we use texts like "we humble our heart in Your presence." Notice that the word "heart" is purposely singular. Members of the congregation may have trouble with this, both for grammatical reasons and because of the individual nature of our society. Since we have given up our individual identities for His body, we now deliberately modify song texts to identify the singularity of His being in the midst of the plurality of our co-operative being. We usually sing about four songs in this section. Though it continues the afterglow established earlier in the praise and worship to Jesus, it may also bring about a second climax and afterglow. Often, though not always, the last song we are likely to sing will be a petition before the Father on behalf of His wife, Israel. [129]

---

[128] John 17:15-21
[129] Exodus 19

The Correlation to the Levitical Offerings

I am always amazed to find continual confirmation and cross referencing throughout the scriptures. Consistent with all biblical truths, this outline for worship can be found in the Torah (books of Moses), and not just in the previously stated arrangement of the Mikdosh. As you can see from the chart below, the five sacrifices identified in the first chapter of Leviticus line up exactly with our outlined approach to the throne of God.

Praise and Worship Outline

Up-tempo praise	Guilt
Humility	Sin
Unity	Peace
Praise/Worship to Jesus	Gift (service/grain)
Praise/Worship to the Father	Burnt
Petition for Israel	

If you follow this outline as shown above it will usually take you between forty-five minutes to an hour. We leave room for the Lord to be Lord in the midst of us, so on occasion we have gone on for an hour and a half. When we meet we allot two hours for our service so if such a thing should occur, the worst thing that happens is that the pastor shortens his talk or postpones it until the following week.

4. A Form for Worship

Binary and Ternary Forms

To further understand the concept of a form for worship we must also understand basic song forms. Song forms have developed as a method of presenting continuity and contrast through the use of repetition and the presentation of music that is different. The two basic song forms are called binary form and ternary form. In binary form there are two melodic statements that are often similar in nature, yet contrasting. The letter "A" represents the first and of course the letter "B" then represents the second. Binary form can be written as "AB" or "AABB" (each statement is repeated). In ternary form there is a restating of the "A" section at the end, so it can be written "ABA" or "AABA." Most hymns in any hymnal follow this form where the first line, second line and fourth line are the same but the third line is uniquely different (ternary form). Piano teachers become acutely aware of this form since students playing a lesson using ternary form after a week of practice seldom are able to play the third line at all, while the other three are seemingly simple. For this reason students have to practice the third line by itself repeatedly.

Song Forms

Binary Form	Ternary Form
AB or AABB	ABA or AABA

Sonata Form

An extension of these forms is called "Sonata" form and is commonly used in the writing of symphonies. Rather than phrases being represented by "A" and "B," entire melodies are represented in this way. The presentation of these two melodies is called the "exposition," since the listener is being exposed to previously unknown music. As the piece progresses, one of those two melodies is developed in such a way that the music increasingly intensifies and results in a climax. This section is then referred to as the "development." Finally repeating a part of the exposition in a minor key and often a somewhat slower tempo completes the work. This section in like fashion is called the "recapitulation."

The same form is used in a well-written short story or novel, but in literature the categories of exposition, development (climax), and conclusion are used. If we consider the intimacy between a husband and wife, we could easily categorize that progression as the expression of the intent to be intimate followed by a development leading to a climax and resulting in an "afterglow" as illustrated below.

Sonata Form

Exposition	Development	Recapitulation
Usually 2 melodies	1 of those developed	Developed melody repeated-minor key
Expression of intention	Intensification resulting in climax	Afterglow

Worship Form

It is not difficult to see the correlation between these forms and that they did not simply come about by chance. Since we are pursuant of a deep and lasting intimacy with the Father we must also consider this form for the progression of songs in worship. Although the initial up-tempo praise songs help us shake off the problems of the day, they also become a part of the initiation of our focus on the Lord, and they become a part of our expression of intent to become intimate with the Lord. Our statements of unity and humility deepen that focus and intent. As we begin to praise Jesus in the following section, it now must be with intent toward a climax. The momentum of the songs must continue to build to the point of a climax. In the afterglow that follows we are completely free. Free to bask in Jesus' presence, and as we continue, free to bask in the presence of the Father. It is here that He heals us and delivers us without us necessarily even knowing that He did so.

PRAISE AND WORSHIP OUTLINE

"Up-tempo" Praise	UP-TEMPO SONG 1 UP-TEMPO SONG 2 UP-TEMPO SONG 3 UP-TEMPO SONG 4 (more if needed)	Expression of Intent
Unity/Humility	UNITY SONG HUMILITY SONG (more if needed)	
Praise/Worship - Jesus	PRAISE TO JESUS SONG 1 PRAISE TO JESUS SONG 2 PRAISE TO JESUS SONG 3 PRAISE TO JESUS SONG 4 WORSHIP JESUS SONG 5 WORSHIP JESUS SONG 6	Development (building momentum) Climax Afterglow
Praise/Worship - Father	WORSHIP THE FATHER SONG 1 WORSHIP THE FATHER SONG 2 WORSHIP THE FATHER SONG 3	(Possibly but not necessarily building to another climax-afterglow)

5. The Lordship of Jesus

Along the way I have encountered a number of people who said that Jesus is Lord of their life, but when confronted by a truth that would set them free, they ignored that truth and chose the teachings of doctrines and "religious practices" (rituals that entrap through familiarity and comfort zones). In reality, the doctrines and religious practices are the lord of their life. An individual makes Jesus Lord of their personal life by recognizing their *inability* to control their own life and choose to give control to Him. As they begin to walk in His lordship, they demonstrate their submission to Him by following His direction and not the direction of their own self-will.[130] If a difficult decision is before them and the direction is not obvious, they fast and pray as they seek His clear communication in making that decision. In this way we walk by faith[131] going from "faith to faith" assignments,[132] being pleasing to God as we live by faith.[133]

The same must be true for the life of the body. A clear example is found in the first century church at Antioch. While the congregation was ministering before the Lord and fasting they received a word concerning Saul (Paul) and Barnabas. They fasted and prayed together again, obviously for confirmation of that word, before sending them out as apostles.[134] This is the first step in making Jesus Lord of a congregation. Business meetings should not be "the majority rules" as is done in a Republic or Democracy. If Jesus has spoken, everyone will be in agreement. If everyone is not in agreement, the congregation may need to fast and seek the Lord again.

---

[130] John 14:15
[131] 2 Corinthians 5:7
[132] Romans 1:17
[133] Hebrews 11:6
[134] Acts 13:1-3

If a congregation says 'Jesus is Lord' of that group, there should be a boldly known "presence" of the resurrected Messiah, Jesus (Yeshua) in the midst of the congregation. The greatest opportunity for His bold manifestation is during worship. Many churches post the statement "Jesus is Lord" on the sign in front of the building. The apparent assumption is that if the name of Jesus is on the sign, Jesus is Lord over the congregation. That statement, at the very least, falls vastly short of our true potential. We make Jesus Lord by humbling ourselves in the Holy Spirit and worshiping as a body in His presence, and as He therefore, being manifested through us, brings forth worship before the Most High God.

> "You also, as living stones, are being built up as a spiritual house for a holy priesthood, to offer up spiritual sacrifices acceptable to God through Jesus Christ." [135]

In other words, In Him we are a living temple bringing sacrifices of praises that are uniquely acceptable to God the Father in Him (Jesus). A congregation must learn to do that under Jesus' headship. Just because someone says 'Jesus is Lord' does not make that a reality to that individual or church any more than saying some rock group "rules." It is a congregational practice that constitutes its very life and being, which is the boldly manifested lordship of Jesus. Each of us, having received individual revelation from Him, has entered into all that Jesus has led us to do as we have been following Him. We will in the end succeed in our faith walk by following Him in the same way. As a congregation worships together under His headship, it will first experience unity, and then it will experience love. Members can all grit their teeth and determine to love each other, but the

---

[135] 1 Peter 2:5

truth is that everyone will quickly run out of the energy to love. As we humble ourselves in the presence of Jesus at the foot of the cross, and as we experience His lordship by the Holy Spirit, then love pours out for one another. Real unity and love come from His lordship, and it is crucial to His ministry in the midst of the congregation.

Lines of Authority

Jesus' lordship will establish lines of authority. It is a part of His nature. The worship experience in the true God, God of Abraham, Isaac, and Jacob (Israel) in His son the Messiah Jesus (Yeshua) will not happen without established and maintained lines of authority. The "praise leader," like all other members of the congregation, must function under the authority of the pastor. The pastor is the appointed shepherd who Jesus placed in that position to protect the congregation. He sees what the needs are (both physically and spiritually) more clearly than anyone else and bears the burden of responsibility before Jesus for the entire congregation. Not functioning under the pastor's authority constitutes rebellion and undermines Jesus' manifestation and lordship. Jesus holds His chosen pastor in very high regard[136] and takes it personally when people rebel to his given authority.[137] The pastor is still accountable to the congregation, as are all members, but bears a greater dimension of responsibility in this regard.

Likewise, in praise and worship, the trained musicians and members of the congregation must function under the direction and authority of the music leader. He should be in that position only because it is evident to all that Jesus

---

[136] Revelation 2:1a
[137] Acts 9:4

put him there. When a musician believes that Jesus wants him in such a position, prayer and fasting is necessary on the part of the entire congregation to discern if it is the will of Jesus, and for two reasons. First, the congregation wants to make sure they have the right person in that position. Second, because that position should never be questioned again. When it is clearly established, everyone must flow under his direction. Often people (even sometimes the trained musicians) say, 'If I have to follow the song leader it impedes my ability to worship.' My response is that if they cannot follow my direction how can we expect to flow into the kind of unity that brings the King into Headship in the midst of the body? Someone has to present the initial direction. If that kind of statement comes from a member of the team (singers or instrumentalists who are up front) they need to leave that post and worship with the congregation until they are able to promote a heart of "oneness" to the congregation. Jesus may have put them in that post, but not for the purpose of being an obstacle for the rest of the musicians or the congregation. Just as musicians must practice to improve, they also must work together toward a unified focus. When that is first established among the team of musicians, it is then "in place" to enable unity for the entire body.

We all recognize that there are very many denominational churches and that there are people who move from church to church, and it is their choice to do so. If, however, a congregation is truly functioning as a body with Jesus as its Head, He has chosen the individual members of it.[138] Every member must have a "word" from Him that He wants him or her to be there. They must then humbly factor into the congregation, seeing themselves as the least of the

---

[138] Matthew 18:20

members.[139] Satan will work relentlessly to undermine and nullify the manifestation of Jesus in the earth. Satan focuses on individual sin and disunity in an effort to accomplish this. Seeing one's self as either unimportant or more important than others can both nullify a member. Looking upon brothers and sisters in the flesh and gossiping can easily cause disunity and division, totally squelching the manifestation of Jesus.

The Importance of Trained Musicians

Well-trained musicians are imperative to the freedom necessary for congregational worship. Members should not have to be concerned about instrumentalists or singers as to whether they can play the music, keep the beat, or just provide the support and structure necessary for worship to happen. The team must be well rehearsed so members of the body are free to be beside themselves in the Holy Spirit. Early in my work with the church a gentleman came in one Sunday morning and asked if he could play along with us on his guitar. Wanting to be nice to him, I agreed. He then brought in an electric guitar with its amplifier and played it so loudly that the rest of us could not even hear ourselves playing our own instruments. This in turn completely squelched the manifestation of Jesus in His body. I determined this (or anything else like it) would never happen again. When people make that offer now, I invite them to our rehearsals and inform them that after a few weeks I might consider allowing them to play for a service with the team. If they are serious, they will come to the rehearsals. If not, the problem is already solved. In this way, I am able to protect the manifestation of Jesus (under the authority of the pastor) within our congregation.

---

[139] Luke 9:48; 1 Corinthians 15:9; Ephesians 3:8

These musicians must also demonstrate stability in their lives and in their families. By taking a position of a certain dimension of leadership, they must function in great unity with the other musicians. This is not possible if their personal lives are in disarray and rehearsals end up becoming group counseling sessions.

Should All Members Be Trained Musicians?

Before you are quick to say 'no', there is a sensitivity that musicians acquire as they are learning an instrument. It is important to the members of the congregation to be sensitive to the Lord and to each other. I personally believe that all talent is a learned behavior. That means that, provided that one is not physically disabled, anyone can learn a musical instrument to some degree of proficiency. The younger we are as we make that venture, the better, but anyone can learn an instrument at any age. I believe that if members of the congregation choose to do so, they may well find themselves functioning better, more freely and more fully in the midst of the congregation. It is a constructive way for members to facilitate worship.

The Importance of Pastoral Participation

Unfortunately there is not a lot of instruction for pastors in the scripture. The word "pastor" literally means, "shepherd." They are, at the same time, members of the body. They should be free to participate in worship and, therefore, also the manifestation of Jesus. As shepherds they are looking out for the well being of the entire congregation and each individual member of it. They are successful if they make Jesus the Lord of their personal life, they enable Jesus to be Lord of the body and they are able to keep anyone else from being Lord of the congregation. In shepherding, they should have direct input on the songs selected for praise and worship. Often pastors are not musicians, which may complicate the process for a time, but the song list should be Jesus' list brought forth through the pastor and music leader/director. This requires a devotion time on the part of those developing that list. As the pastor is continually in prayer for the congregation, his heart is already tuned to the needs of the members and the needs of the Lord as we minister before Him. He is the one who is most sensitive and inclined to what is most appropriate on behalf of all.

6. The Body of the Messiah (Christ)

Many churches have weekly altar calls. When people come up front they are encouraged to confess their sins, which of course is good. They are also told at this point that they are "born again." They surely have made a choice to be a new person and have the opportunity from this point on to "go and sin no more," [140] but Jesus said: *"You did not choose Me but I chose you."* [141] With that in mind let's take a look at what He did say about being born again.

> *Now there was a man of the Pharisees, named Nicodemus, a ruler of the Jews; this man came to Jesus by night and said to Him, "Rabbi, we know that You have come from God as a teacher; for no one can do these signs that You do unless God is with him." Jesus answered and said to him, "Truly, truly, I say to you, unless one is born again he cannot see the kingdom of God." Nicodemus said to Him, "How can a man be born when he is old? He cannot enter a second time into his mother's womb and be born, can he?" Jesus answered, "Truly, truly, I say to you, unless one is born of water and the Spirit he cannot enter into the kingdom of God. That which is born of the flesh is flesh, and that which is born of the Spirit is spirit. Do not be amazed that I said to you, 'You must be born again.' The wind blows where it wishes and you hear the sound of it, but do not know where it comes from and where it is going; so is everyone who is born of the Spirit." Nicodemus said to Him, "How can these things be?" Jesus answered and said to him, "Are you the teacher of Israel and do not understand these things?"* [142]

---

[140] John 8:11
[141] John 15:16a
[142] John 3:1-10

That last statement means Nicodemus should have understood these things. It also means that as he was studying and teaching scripture, what Jesus was speaking about was all over the Hebrew Scriptures (Old Testament). *"Unless one is born again he cannot see* (perceive, understand, discern) *the kingdom of God."* [143] This is also not a statement implying final judgment, but is implying election and its subsequent perception. Before Jesus met me I knew about Him, but I really didn't know Him. I didn't understand what He was doing or why. After He met me, I immediately understood Him and His purposes for me much more fully. As I then studied the scriptures He revealed more and more to me. I identified with others who had similar experiences.

Abram knew nothing about God. Then one day God spoke to him. As a result he dropped everything and followed God to "the land." [144] Isaac witnessed his father being stopped by an angel, as Abram was about to sacrifice him. [145] Surely his eyes were opened and he also perceived the kingdom, as is evident in his life after this revelation. [146] Jacob swindled his brother out of his birthright and his inheritance. Then he had a great dream and saw angels ascending and descending on a ladder that extended into heaven. The Lord also made great promises to him, as He had to his father and grandfather. [147] Still another revelation came to him as he wrestled with "a man" throughout the night before he met his brother. [148] Moses had his revelation experience at the burning bush. [149] Prior to that event

---

[143] John 3:3b
[144] Genesis 12:1-5
[145] Genesis 22:10-12
[146] Genesis 24:63; 25:11; 25:21; 26:24-25
[147] Genesis 28:12-17
[148] Genesis 32
[149] Exodus 3

God was surely directing Moses, but in his own mind he was doing his own thing. After that revelation experience he was completely different, and his goals were conformed to the goals of the Lord. Joshua witnessed quite a lot of the interaction of God with Moses, but also received his own personal revelation before he led the people into the land.[150] It even appears that Jesus (in a separate event) also revealed himself to Joshua before he led Israel into battle at Jericho.[151] Eli (the priest) was given the responsibility of raising Samuel. Even though they were living in the tabernacle (at Shiloh), Samuel did not expect God to speak to him. Then one night Samuel heard his name being called repeatedly and Eli realized that it was God speaking to him.[152] The books of the prophets most often begin with some kind of statement of a vision or revelation experience. These men of Israel all received "born again" experiences and, as a result, were able to perceive what God was doing.

Notice that the rest of the people who did not share their experience were not condemned to hell. This revelation experience is not a requirement for salvation, for *"everyone who calls on the name of the Lord will be saved."*[153]

However, it is a requirement for being a tool in the hand of God in hastening His coming kingdom, and it is a requirement for being a functional member of the body. He chooses those He knows are equipped with the talents to complete His tasks. Although He is the giver of those talents and provides opportunities for training and development, His selection often includes criteria we may not see

---

[150] Joshua 1:1-9
[151] Joshua 5:13-15
[152] 1 Samuel 3
[153] Acts 2:21

or understand. His selection, therefore, may not be apparent to others or ourselves.[154]

The popular Christian band, Casting Crowns, recorded a song a while back called "If We Are the Body." It asks the question, "If we are the body (of 'Christ') why aren't miraculous things happening through us?" There are two potential answers. The one for which they are prodding is that we as the individual members of a congregation are not walking in enough faith or righteousness for those things to be happening. The inconceivable option, which is really the case, is that most of those "churches" are not the body, but just nice social clubs. First, any group that is too large for everyone to know everyone is a social club. Churches where there are multiple services also cannot be a body. If church members are not worshiping in the same room at the same time, then at best they may possibly function as separate bodies. If members decide they cannot attend a service at the regular time and go to another service, they may witness another body, but cannot confess Jesus' lordship in their decision to be there, and so they cannot function as a part of that body. The Lord instructs His body members to be part of a specific body in a specific geographic location and from that time on it is their personal responsibility to faithfully fulfill His purposes for them in that body.

In the end, when we *"go to meet Him in the air"* and *"at the last trumpet"* we will all constitute His collective body, but that will be when He comes. Until then His purposes are fulfilled through local bodies in specific geographic locations. Taking all of that into consideration, let us take a more careful look at these scriptural statements:

---

[154] 1 Samuel 16:7

"For this we say to you by the word of the Lord, that we who are alive and remain until the coming of the Lord, will not precede those who have fallen asleep. For the Lord Himself will descend from heaven with a shout, with the voice of the archangel and with the trumpet of God, and the dead in Christ will rise first. Then we who are alive and remain will be caught up together with them in the clouds to meet the Lord in the air, and so we shall always be with the Lord, ...[155]

"Behold, I tell you a mystery; we will not all sleep, but we will all be changed, in a moment, in the twinkling of an eye, at the last trumpet; for the trumpet will sound, and the dead will be raised imperishable, and we will be changed. For this perishable must put on the imperishable, and this mortal must put on immortality." [156]

Since our God is a consuming fire[157] we can consider His presence similar to and surely greater than the core of a nuclear *fusion* reactor. It must be contained or it would consume everything around it for many miles. It appears that we are given a new creation body and at least one function of that transformation is for us to be the containment unit for the very presence of the glory of God at Jesus' return to the earth. At this point all of the "bodies" that have been spread out around the world will be assembled into one. Collectively they will constitute the house in which He dwells.[158]

---

[155] 1 Thessalonians 4:15-17
[156] 1 Corinthians 15:51-53
[157] Deuteronomy 4:24; 9:3
[158] 1 Peter 2:4-5

Gifts for Advancing the Kingdom

There are specific gifts that we are offered and in fact we are instructed to want.[159] They are very special gifts in the eyes of God. While preaching Jesus said:

> *"So I say to you, ask (or keep asking), and it will be given to you; seek (or keep seeking), and you will find; knock (or keep knocking), and it will be opened to you. For everyone who asks, receives; and he who seeks, finds; and to him who knocks, it will be opened. Now suppose one of you fathers is asked by his son for a fish; he will not give him a snake instead of a fish, will he? Or if he is asked for an egg, he will not give him a scorpion, will he? If you then, being evil, know how to give good gifts to your children,* **how much more will your heavenly Father give the Holy Spirit to those who ask Him?"** [160]*

In order to function as a member of the body and thus, to be a vehicle of Jesus' manifestation you must first be one who is "baptized" or "indwelt" with the Holy Spirit. If you don't ask for this gift you will not just suddenly get it. No one is born with it. After you have asked for it you must exercise faith to believe that God wants you to have it and that He gave it to you when you asked. My earthly father died when I was in college. In dealing with that trauma I read through the New Testament from beginning to end for the first time. When I read the above scripture and saw what it clearly said, I asked for the gift of the Holy Spirit.

---

[159] 1 Corinthians 14:1, 12
[160] Luke 11:9-13

His plan for me was bigger than I could understand, so at that time nothing happened. Thirteen years later He answered that prayer in a powerful way. Looking back, I can see how He used that time to prepare me to meet Him and in the process was preparing me to be a vessel in His hands.

The baptism in water is for repentance. When we go under the water, it is as though our old-self dies and the new person, who now has chosen a life of righteous living, emerges.[161] It also enables us to do battle against the accuser, being in a position to tell him that the one he is accusing was truly guilty, but now is dead and under the water. Baptism in the Holy Spirit would then imply that His Spirit fills our inner being, encompassing every area of our body internally in a like fashion to how the water encompassed every area of our body externally.

There is a purpose in having the baptism of the Holy Spirit. There are nine specific gifts He can give to those who receive this baptism. They are 1) the word of wisdom, 2) the word of knowledge, 3) faith, 4) healing, 5) effecting of miracles, 6) prophecy, 7) distinguishing of spirits, 8) various kinds of tongues and 9) the interpretation of those tongues.[162] As we read through the gospels we clearly see Jesus exercising all of these gifts except the last two. There is either no record of Him doing so or He simply did not use these gifts, since He had no difficulty in expressing Himself to the Father. Since He has now chosen to manifest Himself through bodies of believers it is only natural for us to expect Him to continue His ministry using these gifts that have been given to the individual members of His body. In a larger congregation there will probably be

---

[161] Romans 6:4
[162] 1 Corinthians 12:8-10

many who have the same gift or gifts. He is then free to choose different people at different times to bring forth His manifestation through members of His body.

The Local Body and Denominational Christianity

It should be evident by now that the church assembled by Jesus is remarkably different from modern denominational churches (Presbyterian, Lutheran, Baptist, Catholic, Assembly of God, etc.). The good news is that if scripture is being read, then at least, in part, Jesus is being preached and many are choosing life. The down side, however, is that perhaps many who could and should be participants in His manifestation do not even know where to begin. Without a defined focus, even in congregations that receive the baptism of the Holy Spirit many individuals seek the baptism and subsequent gifts only for the purpose of their own personal gratification. Unfortunately, much of the focus is on the individual.

Again, all of this is not about us. It is about Him. It is all about Him. He delights in our participation, and He drops opportunities right in front of us,[163] but remember that the problem we have from Adam is rebellion and self-focus. Adam and Eve always understood good and evil from God's perspective. He said, 'Don't eat from that tree'[164] (His perspective) and for a time they refrained from doing so. After being tempted with 'becoming wise' (self-focus), they ate from (implying communing with another source) the tree of the knowledge of good and evil.[165] Immediately their focus turned to themselves as they attempted to put

---

[163] Ruth 2:15-16
[164] Genesis 2:16-17
[165] Genesis 3:6

the blame on others.[166]   In our personal lives it should always be our goal to be selfless and keep our focus on Jesus,[167] His kingdom and His righteousness.[168] Serving the body helps us to keep that focus. It is important to the life of a congregation to have some social time, but this should not give way to social programs (Mom's day out, aerobics classes, etc.) that focus on the individual "needs" (actually "wants") of the members. He does not mind that you enjoy the gift(s) He gave you, but His gifts are for the purpose of enabling you to be a vehicle of His manifestation in His body, through which He is, therefore, manifested in the earth.

A true church ("local body") is not an organization, but an organism. Denominational Christianity can never fulfill the posture of being a local church (with Jesus as their Head) since they take their direction from the denomination. In simpler terms, if the government of the denomination is determining what that church believes and does, the denominational government is the Lord of that congregation, and, therefore, Jesus is not.

---

[166] Genesis 3:12-13
[167] John 3:14
[168] Matthew 6:33

7. Unity in the Body

Without unity in the body all manifestations of the Messiah will be at best very strained. During His last evening with his disciples Jesus taught and prayed with them. A great portion of His prayer dealt with this issue of unity. Here is what He said:

> "As You sent Me into the world, I also have sent them into the world. For their sakes I sanctify Myself, that they themselves also may be sanctified in truth. I do not ask on behalf of these alone, but for those also who believe in Me through their word; that they may all be one; even as You, Father, are in Me and I in You, that they also may be in Us, so that the world may believe that You sent Me. The glory which You have given Me I have given to them, that they may be one, just as We are one; I in them and You in Me, that they may be perfected in unity, so that the world may know that You sent Me, and loved them, even as You have loved Me." [169]

Since Jesus knew that the following day He would be hanging on the cross we can safely assume that His focus was on what was really important to this core group. He understood that it would be foundational to the church birthed seven weeks later at Pentecost (Shavuot). Some years later the apostle Paul, who was working at the development of other new congregations and thus observing Jesus working within those bodies, had this to say to the church at Corinth:

---

[169] John 17:18-23

> *"For even as the body is one and yet has many members, and all the members of the body, though they are many, are one body, so also is Christ. For by one Spirit we were all baptized into one body, whether Jews or Greeks, whether slaves or free, and we were all made to drink of one Spirit. For the body is not one member, but many."* [170]

Paul begins (Chapter twelve) by explaining these spiritual gifts (gifts of the Holy Spirit) and how they are used in the assembly of the Body; how each part of the Body is important to the wholeness of Jesus' expression. Then he embarks onto an entire chapter (the famous chapter thirteen) on the topic of love. It is often read at weddings and special occasions, but Paul is not talking about romantic love (even though what he says still applies). He is speaking about our relationship to one another in the "body." This love is not physical but is committed to standing shoulder to shoulder with one another until He comes. This is evidenced by the fact that in the following chapter (fourteen) he returns to the topic of the orderly and edifying use of these spiritual gifts.

A statement the apostle Paul makes to the churches of Galatia that is hardly ever seen is this:

> *"My children, with whom I am again in labor until Christ (the Messiah) is formed in you-"* [171]

There is a reason for why it is missed. It doesn't appear to be that important. But the word "formed" in the original

---

[170] 1 Corinthians 12:12-14
[171] Galatians 4:19

Greek text is μορφόω (morpho-o) and literally means to be "morphed" or changed in shape or form. Paul is saying that the assembled body is eventually morphed into a body through which Jesus himself is manifested in the earth.

To the church in Rome, Paul wrote:

> *"Now may the God who gives perseverance and encouragement grant you to be of the same mind with one another according to Christ Jesus, so that with one accord you may with **one voice** glorify the God and Father of our Lord Jesus Christ."* [172]

Here Paul is recognizing a true phenomenon. How can an assembly of multiple individuals become one voice? Choral directors also pursue a similar goal. If a singing group is truly unified, though there are often thirty- (or more) individuals in a choir (chorus), the goal is to communicate the song as one voice. Even though it is the goal, it is not possible for any of us to achieve perfection in this flesh, and even more than one person compounds that fact.

The first difficulty is a balance of sound. Since basic choral groups divide into four parts, there should be the same volume of sound coming from each section with a slightly greater volume from the part carrying the melody. This begins with the same (or close to the same) number of people in each section. Most often more women than men choose to participate, so this is often a difficulty. While working to achieve a balance of sound, the greater challenge is blend. The ultimate goal is for every singer to breathe (support the tone) the same way and to use their voice in the same way, shaping their mouth with a raised

---

[172] Romans 15:5-6

soft pallet and depressed tongue while directing the breath to the teeth and in the process further unifying the tone by shaping "round vowels." From the audience every mouth should have a rounded shape that is taller than wide. Each of these focuses requires a great deal of time to develop in the understanding and habitual use of each singer. Instructors have to introduce each concept individually (to avoid confusion) and from many different angles. Invariably there are singers in the group who study with private voice teachers. You would like to think that would help, but all those teachers have different approaches to their instruction, and; very frankly, many of them actually don't know what they are doing, all of which further complicates achieving the goal of "one voice."

In the congregation there is a place for that well-trained group of singers, instrumentalists, or dancers. Their presentations are as an offering before the Lord and for the edification of the body. Body members should be able to continue in a heart of worship while a presentation is being offered. Like the Levitical offerings they should be the best of the flock, without blemish.[173] Our presentations that are offerings to Him should be as polished as we are able to present.

The "one voice" Paul is speaking about, however, is different. It may be as difficult to procure and it surely requires spiritual discernment to hear. It is not a quality of the music. When the king is in the camp, there is a unified focus. If individuals speak, read scripture, pray, or manifest gifts of the Spirit, all of it goes in the same direction, His direction. All participants experience His presence and their hearts are melted by it. He ministers as He chooses

---

[173] Exodus 29:1; Ezekiel 43:22-25; 45:18-23; 46:4-6, 13; Hebrews 9:14

and love freely abounds among the body members. Jesus ushers His body before the Father and we are free to worship the Father in Him as He worships the Father in us.

For those who have never experienced this, it is scary. Getting intimate like this with the Father surely means being naked (fully exposed) before Him. Frankly speaking we are fully exposed before Him continually, but in this environment many fear He may speak to them, and frankly He might just do that. God is not a magician. Those who do not seek intimacy with Him in this age will not magically do so in the age to come. If you are reading this and are really uncomfortable right now, He is calling you. Do not hold back anything from Him. He is a refined gentleman who will not violate you. Make everything right with Him so that you may approach His throne of grace boldly.

> *"For the word of God is living and active and sharper than any two-edged sword, and piercing as far as the division of soul and spirit, of both joints and marrow, and able to judge the thoughts and intentions of the heart. And there is no creature hidden from His sight, but all things are open and laid bare to the eyes of Him with whom we have to do. Therefore, since we have a great high priest who has passed through the heavens, Jesus the Son of God, let us hold fast our confession. For we do not have a high priest who cannot sympathize with our weaknesses, but One who has been tempted in all things as we are, yet without sin. Therefore let us draw near with confidence to the throne of grace, so that we may receive mercy and find grace to help in time of need."* [174]

---

[174] Hebrews 4:12-16

Jesus said that He does what He sees His Father doing.[175] Before I was baptized in the Holy Spirit I could not see what the Father was doing. With Jesus as the Head of a body, members should also be able to see what the Father is doing. So what is the Father doing?

---

[175] John 5:19-20

8. What is the Father Doing?

About a quarter of the entire bible is written by prophets. Much of what they have written tells us what is still going to happen. I am often amazed at the Christians who are drawn in droves to Prophecy Conferences to hear some new prophetic word, when few, if any, actually know what the prophets themselves said. Although they may focus on different aspects, the prophets all write repeatedly about five primary themes. They are:

1. The Regathering of the People of Israel
   back to the Land of Israel
2. The Great King
3. God's Glory in Zion
4. The Judgment of the Nations
5. The New Creation

This is a rather clear picture of what the Father is doing. God is "cleaning up the spill," not just from the fall of Adam and Eve but also from the fall of Satan.[176] He is using His chosen vessels to bring all rebellion into one place (Armageddon) so that He can judge it. The people of Israel were first in the land to present a picture of the Kingdom of God on a small scale under the rule of, first, King David and then his son Solomon. Following the Babylonian captivity they returned for a short time for the life and ministry of Jesus the Messiah. Again they were dispersed, both times as judgment for error[177] but also bearing the message 'if God will judge His people, He will also judge the nations.' Now, two thousand years later they have miraculously returned to the land again.

---

[176] Ezekiel 28:12-19
[177] Ezekiel 36:19; Zechariah 2:6

Speaking about the people of Israel to the newly established church in Rome the apostle Paul said,

> *"For if their rejection is the reconciliation of the world, what will their acceptance be but life from the dead?"* [178]

Israel has been re-established as a nation since 1948 and the Temple Mount (Mount Moriah and Mount Zion) was temporarily delivered in 1967 fulfilling at least, in part, what Jesus himself prophesied when he said,

> *"...and they will fall by the edge of the sword, and will be led captive into all the nations; and Jerusalem will be trampled under foot by the Gentiles until the times of the Gentiles are fulfilled."* [179]

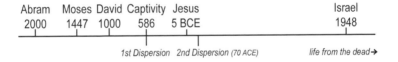

We don't know the day or the hour,[180] but we are required to see the signs of the times and know we are drawing near to the coming of the king and the establishment of the kingdom of God on the earth.[181] God is a Zionist.[182] He is the one who is polarizing the nations.

We also know from Jesus' parable of the dragnet[183] (the

---

[178] Romans 11:15
[179] Luke 21:24
[180] Mark 13:32
[181] Mark 13:28-29
[182] Psalm 132:13
[183] Matthew 13:47-50

intersecting points of the net being local churches) that He is working at placing an organism of His manifestation in or near every major city in the world.

Much of what the Father is doing can be discerned in the Spirit, especially in the midst of the body.

Paul exhorts the body at Corinth in this way:

> "...For to us God revealed them through the Spirit; for the Spirit searches all things, even the depths of God. For who among men knows the thoughts of a man except the spirit of the man which is in him? Even so the thoughts of God no one knows except the Spirit of God. Now we have received, not the spirit of the world, but the Spirit who is from God, so that we may know the things freely given to us by God, which things we also speak, not in words taught by human wisdom, but in those taught by the Spirit, combining spiritual thoughts with spiritual words." [184]

We are actually able to discern the mind of God through His Holy Spirit. All of what we perceive will be substantiated in the scripture, so it is important for us to know, as much as possible, what the bible says. We must also be able to find confirmation and in multiple witnesses,[185] which can also be defined as not just finding one obscure verse, but multiple scriptures clearly reinforcing that word. John encourages us to not believe every spirit (every thought that enters your head) but to test them to see if they are from God.[186]

---

[184] 1 Corinthians 2:10-13
[185] Deuteronomy 17:6; 19:15; Matthew 18:16; 2 Corinthians 13:1; 1 Timothy 5:19; Hebrews 10:28
[186] 1 John 4:1-3

I recently experienced a revealing vision. I was accompanying a tour group in Israel and was functioning as the song leader for the group. About a third of the group was from our congregation. I was buffeted by the enemy for weeks before the trip and believed that when I finally got to the airport, the battle for it would be over. It took me twelve hours however to get to New York and then we sat on the tarmac for over an hour before take-off. Not a full week into the tour I broke a tooth and it abscessed. Something was going on I was not seeing. I lost a day from the group seeing a dentist and getting antibiotics. The next day I was able to rejoin the group for the city tour through Jerusalem.

We began the day on top of the Mount of Olives, looking over Jerusalem and specifically the Temple Mount. We discussed biblical things from that visual perspective. From there we traveled down the "Palm Sunday Road" and at the bottom of the mountain went into the Garden of Gethsemane. Then, as we were facing the closed up Eastern Gate, we walked along the road to the north and entered into the Arab quarter of the old city through the Lion's Gate. Since this was my fifth trip to Israel I was seeing and understanding things I had not previously realized. We continued up the hill (the north side of Mount Moriah) and when we came to the top we turned off to the right where we entered Saint Anne's Monastery. As we entered into the church building we saw that there was a group already in there, along with a number of people who were not with any group. They were already singing "The Lord's Prayer," so we joined in with them. Our group sat on the "audience left" side since there was more room there. I determined that I would lead them in the traditional "a capella" Hallelujah, since it just says Hallelujah over and over and is easy for anyone to learn 'on the fly.' I waited for the other group to finish and started this song.

Saint Anne's is a Roman-built church that is an acoustic disaster, but it is still fun to sing there, because it just keeps "ringing." So I led them through the first phrase and then actually conducted a cut off so they could "let it ring." When I started the second phrase I felt like there were beings in the room singing with us that we could not see. I looked to my left and realize that, in addition to that, the other group had started exactly the same song at exactly the same time in exactly the same key at exactly the same tempo. This phenomenon is not possible in human terms and I instantly realized that Jesus was there, had taken His position as our head and was being manifested in the midst of us. The worship was short, but frankly even more breath taking than what I usually had experienced back home with our congregation.

We continued out to the pool of Bethesda, and then to the site of the Roman Street on which Jesus must have walked, carrying His cross to the site of His execution. Traveling down the Via Dolorosa (Street of Agony) we then crossed through the Arab market into the Jewish quarter where we ate a late lunch. We continued walking down to the Western Wall, then out the Dung Gate to the ruins of the City of David. The last part of that tour is to go through Hezekiah's Tunnel. In order to pass through that tunnel you have to walk through water, and since I had not brought shorts or swimming trunks, I opted out of that part of the tour, as did some others. We sat down to wait for the others to come out. When they did, I rose to walk but began to slide sideward down the mountainside. Even though I was on a paved trail, there was gravel under my feet and I just kept sliding. I tried to sit, but completely lost footing from my right leg. My left leg snapped before I could get to the ground. Both tibia and fibula had fractured with a split down the tibia into the "ball and socket" of the ankle. As I lay there I asked the Lord, "Why did this happen?" I immediately had a vision.

I saw Satan being withheld by two very large heavenly beings. The scenario was similar to that of King David in 1 Chronicles 21. David had taken a census, which was a sin for him. He was measuring the strength of his army in the number of soldiers he had rather than trusting in the strength of the Lord. So the Lord sent a pestilence against Israel, 70,000 men of Israel fell.

> *"Then David lifted up his eyes and saw the angel of the LORD standing between earth and heaven, with his drawn sword in his hand stretched out over Jerusalem."* [187]

In my vision these three spiritual entities were literally standing in the same location, and between earth and heaven. Satan's battle was against them. It was not against me. Then very suddenly Satan threw a cheap shot at me and struck me with his sword.

---

[187] 1 Chronicles 21:16a

I had an angel that was covering me, but Satan struck me at an uncovered place, my left lower leg and ankle. I was shocked and immediately thought to myself, "Why would Satan choose to attack me personally?" I know there are people who think they are a threat to Satan, but they really are not. What is truly threatening to him is Jesus being manifested through a body of people. Thoughts were racing through my mind, but the Lord directed my thinking to earlier in the day and the worship time we had shared at Saint Anne's. Although that place is not within the Temple Mount complex, it is still on Mount Moriah, the place where the Lord told Abraham that He would see eternally. This place is where God put His name. Solomon petitioned God that if anyone looks toward the mountain when praying God would hear his prayer.[188] It is the only acceptable location of the altar, which was not revealed to Moses,[189] but later

---

[188] 1 Kings 8; 2 Chronicles 6
[189] Deuteronomy 12:21; 26:2

was revealed to King David.[190] The Mosque now seated on the mountain is the "Abomination that makes Desolate." The prophet Daniel tells us,

> *"Forces from him will arise, desecrate the sanctuary fortress, and do away with the regular sacrifice. And they will set up the abomination of desolation."* [191]

And in the next chapter he tells us,

> *"From the time that the regular sacrifice is abolished and the abomination of desolation is set up, there will be 1,290 days."* [192]

If the days Daniel is speaking of are actually years, then from the time of Daniel and his writing that would bring us to the early 700's A.D., which is when the Mosque of Omar (Dome of the Rock) was built. The Islamic presence on the mountain obstructs the presence of the God of Israel from that place, the place from which the Messiah Jesus (Y'shua or Yahoshua) will rule over the nations of the whole earth. I realized we had just gone into Saint Anne's and had done what we do every weekend in our congregation. Because of the geographic location of this occurrence, I was able to see that Satan was losing his grip. He was not going to be able to keep the Lord off of His "Holy Mountain" much longer. Through the prophet Gad, King David was instructed to make a sacrifice on the mountain to stop the pestilence. This is not just any mountain. Abraham brought Isaac to this mountain to sacrifice him there. The temple was later built in this place. After the Babylonians destroyed the first temple a second was built in the same place years later. Jesus was crucified and resurrected, if

---

[190] 1 Chronicles 21
[191] Daniel 11:31
[192] Daniel 12:11

not on, then very close to this mountain. Jesus ascended into heaven across the valley from this mountain. When He returns, He comes back in exactly the same pattern from which He left. He returns to that mountain for the purpose of ruling over the whole earth from it. This is THE MOUNTAIN. David bought the mountain from its owner, who was willing to give it away to help out, but David said,

> "No, but I will surely buy it for the full price; for I will not take what is yours for the LORD, or offer a burnt offering which costs me nothing." [193]

So King David bought the Temple Mount. It therefore belongs to Israel. He then made a sacrifice on the mountaintop and fire came down from heaven and consumed the sacrifice.[194] David then had a great revelation from God. As a result of all of this he declared,

> "This is the house of the LORD God, and this is the altar of burnt offering for Israel." [195]

Following this David instructed Solomon to build the stone temple in that place, because God had revealed that this was the place! What Satan had meant for evil God had turned to good.[196] For me, no one wants a broken leg, but I now understand the importance of the geographic location of the Temple Mount, both to the Lord and to His/our enemy. This area of land referred to as the "occupied west bank" (of Jordan) is really Judea and Samaria, the biblical heartland of Israel. It is what Jacob declared to be the gate of Heaven,[197] implying it to be the crossing over place between heaven and earth.

---

[193] 1 Chronicles 21:24b
[194] 1 Chronicles 21:26
[195] 1 Chronicles 22:1
[196] Romans 8:28
[197] Genesis 28:17

9. Conclusion

What have we been missing? It is really more of an issue of how things got off track and how we can get back to where we were supposed to be all along. Interestingly the path back has always been there, but there is a perfect timing to everything God does, so we can safely assume it is His will for our time. Since it was lost, there has been a gradual return orchestrated by His hand. Martin Luther and the subsequent Protestant Reformation made the first big step. The Azusa Street Movement brought even more revelation, which later blossomed into the Charismatic movement of the 1970's, but the time has surely come for His church to seriously draw near and greatly advance His coming kingdom in the process.

Unfortunately we are able to make ourselves unattractive to Him, and there is nothing Satan would like more than to nullify us and stop Jesus' manifestation through us. When I teach voice lessons, the first and most important thing I instruct a student to do is stop the behaviors that injure or abuse the voice. Before we can worship we also individually must stop behaviors that would prevent Jesus from coming into our midst. The apostle Paul tells the church at Corinth to remove a member from among their midst because he was engaging in an immoral practice that was not even acceptable outside the church, having relations with his father's wife. Paul tells them to

> *"deliver such a one to Satan for the destruction of his flesh, so that his spirit may be saved in the day of the Lord Jesus."* [198]

---

[198] 1 Corinthians 5:1-5

If we assume that it was his stepmother, this may seem to many to be a rather harsh punishment and it would probably be difficult to find even a few churches that would follow that biblical directive today. In addition to pursuing the destruction of this man's flesh so that his spirit might be saved, Paul was actually protecting the manifestation of Jesus in that church. Such a sin would be detestable in Jesus' sight. If the congregation knew of this sin (and they did) and nothing was done about it, Jesus would not come into the assembly any longer. Without most of the members perhaps even seeing it, the church would quickly default to just another religious institution, and some other 'Jesus' would take over and be manifested.

Other difficulties that would be odious to Jesus would be the "baggage" many just seem to hold onto. Unworthiness, fear, rejection, the fear of rejection, bitterness and the huge list of similar "attitudes" are not who we are called to be in Jesus and subsequently will limit our effectiveness in the body. He has called us to His purposes and is fully able and willing to deliver us from these attitudes that we might bear much good fruit.[199] If we diligently seek Him, the reality of His life being manifested in the body[200] will deliver us and will continue to deliver us from these (and other) attitudes as He reaffirms our adoption by His presence in our midst.[201]

In our American culture "unyielded rights" can be a huge problem in the body. We have been taught since early childhood that we have rights, even "human rights." When Jesus met us and we saw the reality of who we really are in the face of who He really is, we realized our inability to save ourselves. By accepting His justification and Lordship, and

---

[199] Matthew 3:11; John 15:2
[200] 2 Corinthians 4:10-11
[201] Romans 8:15

in the process relinquishing our deception of control, we gave up all "rights." We would like everyone to respect us and deal justly with us (especially within the body), but everyone is not at the same place in their walk in Him. We may have to wait on Him to show some their error. In the process we have to humbly and diligently maintain clear and "logless" eyes.[202] Knowing the human condition we should not be surprised when humans are self-oriented. Again, if they continue to seek Him, Jesus will eventually deliver them.

Other problematic conditions include an unwillingness to submit to authority, religion (tools people use to get to God), self-focus, making excuses and blaming others for our errors. These things are also offensive to Him. If you were going on a date would you put on a suit or nice dress and not wash your body? Every individual member of the body must not only be clean, but also confident of their cleanness. We want to be attractive to Him. We want Him to desire us. As a wife makes herself attractive to her husband, we can also make ourselves attractive to Jesus. This is not achieved with fine clothing, jewelry, grooming and pampering, but through humility and unity. We must be as sensitive as we can be both to His presence and to each other. Our mental focus must not be self-oriented, but body oriented. Individually we must freely abandon ourselves to be drunk in the Holy Spirit.[203] We also have to trust Him that as the Holy Spirit is manifested in us; He will use us in ways that are edifying to the entire body as well as ourselves. Finally, we must have the faith to know that as Jesus is manifested in us He will advance His soon-coming kingdom through us. Jesus' message of the Kingdom of God is that there is a King, He is coming to planet earth and He is bringing the Kingdom of God with

---

[202] Matthew 6:22-23; 7:3-5; Luke 6:41-42
[203] Ephesians 5:18

Him. When He does so, His Kingdom will encompass earth and heaven (both the physical and spiritual realms). He will rule over all the earth from Jerusalem; specifically the Temple Mount (also known as Mt. Moriah and Mt. Zion).

The goal is fire and smoke! Every time God the Father intervenes physically in the earth it causes a reaction that produces fire and smoke. God approached Abram through a *"smoking oven and a flaming torch."* [204] Moses met God at the bush that was burning, yet was not being consumed by the fire. [205] Israel as a nation met God at Mount Sinai and there was thunder, lightning, the sound of a trumpet, and the mountain was smoking. [206] When Moses completed building the tabernacle and placed everything in its correct place, the whole tabernacle was filled with smoke so that Moses could not go into the tent. [207] When Solomon completed the Temple in Jerusalem the same phenomena occurred again. [208] The cloud and the brightness of the glory of the Lord identify His manifestation brought forth between the wings of the cherubim on the Ark of the Covenant! [209] Jesus said that when He comes again it will be in the glory of the Father, in clouds of glory (smoke). [210] When the true church meets Jesus in the air, it's within those clouds. [211] In the book of Revelation we even see the Temple in Heaven filled with smoke from His glory. [212] Is it possible that we could get so intimate with Him in worship that the room we are in would become filled with this smoke? We may have to wait until we are gathered with

---

[204] Genesis 15:17
[205] Exodus 3:2-4
[206] Exodus 19:18; 20:18
[207] Exodus 40: 34-35
[208] 2 Chronicles 7:1-2
[209] Exodus 25:22; Ezekiel 10:4
[210] Matthew 24:30; 26:64; Mark 13:26; 14:62
[211] 1 Thessalonians 4:17
[212] Revelation 15:8

Him at Mount Zion,[213] and we may not. Worship of this nature surely advances His kingdom, while at the same time it weakens the enemy's stronghold on the earth.

As I mentioned in the beginning of this book, Handel's oratorio "The Messiah" begins (after the overture) with a tenor recitative that quotes the prophet Isaiah:

> *"The voice of him that crieth in the wilderness, prepare ye the way of the LORD, make straight in the desert a highway for our God."* [214]

I always wondered what people could do to prepare the way of the Lord. Here it is! Be a member of a body that brings forth His manifestation in the earth! Every entity that brings forth His manifestation further weakens Satan's grip on the kingdoms of this world. I am confident those congregations that faithfully avail themselves to His inhabitation He will be manifested through, even on the Temple Mount in Jerusalem. In preparing the way of the Lord we also must understand the Temple Mount itself is an issue for those who have been called to draw near. I believe that when Jesus was manifested in our tour group at Saint Anne's Monastery on the north side of Temple Mount (also known as Mount Moriah and Mount Zion) that the pillars of Satan's kingdom were seriously crumbling. Surely the currently prevailing principality, the dragon of Islam, was reeling about in great distress, simply unable to continue to keep Jesus' presence away any longer. This may have been the first time His presence was known in that critical location since Jesus physically walked this earth. With Jesus going before us, being manifested through perhaps different bodies repeatedly, we can

---

[213] Revelation 14:1
[214] Isaiah 40:3

provide Him with an even bolder expression of His presence on His Holy Hill, preparing the way of the Lord. We must not take rest for ourselves *"and give Him no rest until He establishes and makes Jerusalem a praise in the earth."*[215] Jerusalem is and always has been a reproach to the nations of the earth. What will make her praise worthy in their sight can only be the real King seated on His throne, the throne of His earthly father King David, ruling over the nations of the earth.

If you embark on this path you will experience absolutely awesome, breathtaking intimacy; first with Jesus and then with the Father. Deliverance, healing, prophecy and many other great things may just happen because Jesus is actually physically present, standing within the room through the congregation, His body. In the bible these things happened on occasion even when Jesus was not directly involved. When David was a young man he played his harp and King Saul was delivered from an evil spirit.[216] When Moses died, his eyes were good and he had the virility of a young man because he had spent a great deal of time directly in the presence of God and was constantly being healed by being there.[217] The prophet Elisha, when asked to make a prophecy about a war, called for a minstrel (musician). While he played, the hand of the Lord came upon Elisha and he was able to prophecy.[218] How much more then can we expect with our precious King standing in the midst of us!

As wonderful as all that is, when we physically stand before Him on Mount Zion, all that we have known will be dwarfed by sitting at His feet in the fully revealed and fully mani-

---

[215] Isaiah 62:6-7
[216] 1 Samuel 16:23
[217] Deuteronomy 34:5-7
[218] 2 Kings 3:14-15

fested kingdom of God established on the earth. As Jesus is manifested through bodies in various locations, He will work diligently toward that end, and allow us to participate in the process. Our God is God!

Bibliography

Dr. James Strong, John R. Kohlenberger III, James A. Swanson, *The Strongest Strong's Exhaustive Concordance of the Bible,* Zondervan, Grand Rapids, Michigan 49530

Donald Jay Grout, *A History of Western Music,* W. W. Norton & Company, Inc. New York, 1973

Percy Alfred Scholes, *The Oxford Companion to Music - Tenth Edition,* Oxford University Press, London, England 1975

Willi Apel, *Harvard Dictionary of Music - second Edition,* Harvard University Press, Cambridge, Massachusetts, 1969

R. R. Donnelley & Sons, *Webster's Seventh New Collegiate Dictionary,* G. & C. Merriam Company, Springfield, Massachusetts, 1967

Wikimedia Foundation, Inc., *Wikipedia.com,* Wikimedia Foundation, Inc., 149 New Montgomery St., 3rd Floor, San Francisco, California 94105

Index

comfort - 1, 58
commune(d) - 5, 24
communication - 5, 58
congregation(s) - 1, 2, 3, 10, 11, 12, 13, 20, 39, 44, 48, 49, 50, 51, 52,
    53, 58, 59, 60, 61, 62, 63, 64, 68, 71, 72, 73, 74, 77, 83, 84, 87, 90,
    93, 94
correlation - 54, 57
Corinth - 9, 74, 82, 89
counterfeit - 5, 15
covenant - 1, 23, 28, 36, 92
Creator - 16, 46
cross - 53, 54, 60, 74, 84
Dagon - 34
David - 1, 17, 33, 34, 35, 36, 37, 38, 39, 40, 46, 48, 80, 84, 85, 87, 88,
    94
Davidic - 38, 39
denomination(s) - 14, 73
denominational - 31, 61, 72, 73
development - 9, 13, 19, 56, 67, 74
director(s) - 12, 14, 52, 64, 76
discern - 10, 15, 51, 61, 66, 82
discerned - 82
discerning - 52
discernment - 77
disciples - 41, 42, 74
disunity - 18, 62
dragnet - 10, 81
edification - 77
edify - 18, 50, 52
edifying - 75, 91
Egypt - 23, 26
elder(s) - 6, 7, 34, 52
elect - 50
election - 66, 67
Elisha - 94
encourage(s) - 16, 48, 49. 52, 82
encouraged - 65
encouraging - 13
encouragement - 76
environment - 14, 78
Ephesus - 20
Esau - 25
experience - 1, 2, 3, 4, 5, 6, 8, 16, 22, 26, 46, 59, 60, 66, 67, 77, 94
experienced - 4, 8, 78, 83, 84
experiences - 66, 67

Further Information

If you have questions regarding any of the subjects covered in this book, or if you desire to learn more about the implementation of the concepts presented in this book, you may contact us at the following address:

Fellowship Church
P.O. Box 181191
Casselberry, Florida 32718

You may also contact us via email at:
jim@FaceOfGodmusic.com
or visit our web site at http://FaceOfGodmusic.com